Iowa's Country Schools
Landmarks of Learning

William L. Sherman
Editor

D1379648

Iowa's Country Schools
Landmarks of Learning

William L. Sherman
Editor

Iowa State Education Association
and
Mid-Prairie Books
1998

Front cover: *Arbor Day* by Grant Wood. Reproduced with permission of the Cedar Rapids Community School District.

Front cover: Photograph of Rowley School, Independence School District, by Dave Gosch. Reproduced with permission of the *Cedar Rapids Gazette*.

Back cover: *End of the Day* by P. Buckley Moss. Reproduction of the image and the P. Buckley Moss signature logo with permission of The Moss Portfolio.

First Edition, 1998

Printed in the United States of America.

Book composition by Ireland Design & Publishing, Cedar Falls, Iowa

Published by:
Mid-Prairie Books
P.O. Box 680
Parkersburg IA 50665
(319) 346-2048

Library of Congress #98-065957

ISBN 0-931209-73-0

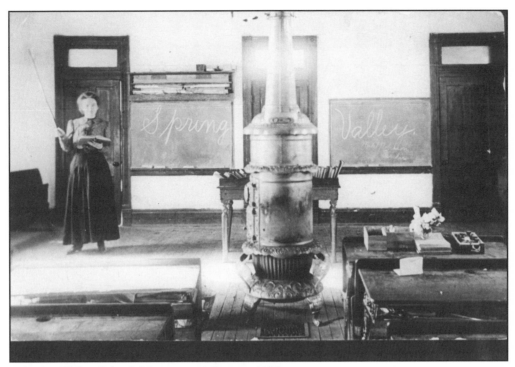

Spring Valley School, Montgomery County, 1890s

Dedication

This book is dedicated to the thousands of men and women who taught in Iowa's one-room schools. Their hard work and sacrifices provided generations of students with educational experiences which helped them become productive citizens and helped Iowa achieve the highest literacy rate in the nation. These teachers made Iowa a leader in learning.

Prine School, Mahaska County, Reenactment, 1975

Acknowledgements

Several individuals have made significant contributions to make this book possible. First and foremost were the local volunteers who worked in counties throughout Iowa to update information about one-room country schools. I estimate that more than 500 persons spent countless hours compiling information and providing a photographic record about country schools in their county. These local volunteers worked without compensation. These people care deeply about the legacy of the one-room school. Without their efforts, this book would not have been possible.

Information from the county volunteers has been turned over to the State Historical Society of Iowa in Des Moines. An archival area on country schools, organized by county, will now be on file for future review and research. The fact that state historical staff members agreed to retain the material collected for this book was a powerful motivator which encouraged many local volunteers to put forth the effort to make this statewide collection possible. Several staff members of the State Historical Society of Iowa offices in Des Moines and Iowa City helped obtain rare photographs and articles about country schools. And the Iowa Historical Foundation provided a grant to help defray some of the expense involved with research and production of the book.

Some of Iowa's best photographers provided a wide range of current and historic photographs that added greatly to this book. They include Bob Nandell, Des Moines; Mike Whye, Council Bluffs; Jolene Rosauer, Cedar Falls; John Deason, Muscatine; Denny Rehder, Des Moines; and Wilford Yoder of Kalona. Many of the local volunteers also provided outstanding current and past photographs of country schools in their county. Most noteworthy was the contribution made by Jack Grandgeorge of Fort Dodge. Jack attended a one-room country school in Webster County. From 1975-85, he photographed every one-room school he saw in travels throughout Iowa and southern Minnesota. He turned over his collection of more than 70 photographs for us to use.

Many Iowa-area newspapers helped us recruit local volunteers by running stories about this project. Several provided photographs. Many wrote feature stories about information compiled by local county volunteers.

Iowa State Education Association Executive Director Fred Comer and President Bob Gilchrist supported this project and allowed me to work on the book. One of ISEA's dedicated secretaries, Cheri Swanson, helped in many ways to keep this project moving forward. Funding from the ISEA/NEA Member Benefits program administered by Bill Pritchard, associate executive director for administration for ISEA, helped make possible a statewide distribution of this book to local ISEA affiliates.

Publication of this book would not have been attempted without the backing and support of Robert Neymeyer, publisher of Mid-Prairie Books. Bob said yes to an idea without seeing any copy. He and his colleagues worked hard on tight timelines to bring the book through the publication process.

Bill Dreier, Professor Emeritus at the University of Northern Iowa, agreed to provide a historical overview of Iowa's one-room schools. He spent several hours developing an article, and we jointly developed the first timeline of important dates for Iowa's one-room schools. Bill also contributed to the Black Hawk County report.

Nancy Barry, Associate Professor of English at Luther College, contributed a significant article that, for the first time, defines the impact one-room schools have had and are continuing to have on Iowa education. Both Nancy and Bill agreed to contribute to this project with only a promise they would receive a complimentary book several months down the road.

Others who provided valuable information were Steve Johnson and Erik Ericksen. Johnson produced drawings of one-room school building designs, and Ericksen shared insights on how religious groups are maintaining one-room school traditions.

Another organization that helped find county volunteers when earlier recruitment efforts failed was the Iowa Genealogical Society. Without their help, a complete county summary would not have been possible.

Paintings from two artists enhance this book. John Fitzpatrick, fine arts coordinator for the Cedar Rapids School District, helped obtain use of the Grant Wood *Arbor Day* painting which appears on the front cover.

Four paintings created by P. Buckley Moss are also used to enhance this book. These include: *End of the Day,* a painting of the Cedar Falls Little Red Schoolhouse that appears on the back cover. Three paintings produced by Moss that appear inside the book include: *Grant Wood School,* located in Jones County near Anamosa; *School Picnic,* located in Polk County at Living History Farms; and *The Birthplace of the 4-H Emblem* of the Breckenridge School now located in Clarion in Wright County. The Moss paintings are used with permission granted by Laura Black of The Moss Portfolio.

Another significant piece of artwork included in the book is "The Family Circus" cartoon of a country school scene released to newspapers on September 5, 1993. This cartoon is reprinted with special permission of the King Features Syndicate.

Several other companies gave us permission to reproduce items. They are noted on the pages where these items are printed. We are grateful for the permission to use this artwork.

Joe Millard also made a significant contribution. He coordinated the collection of information about Jefferson County schools and provided a copy of the 1890 test given to eighth graders attending country schools in Iowa. Check and see how many of these questions you can answer.

Mary Jo Bruett of the Iowa Department of Education helped us obtain the statistical information about education at the turn of the century. She also provided some photographs and gave us assistance in locating information about other publications dealing with one-room schools.

Several others were helpful and encouraged us to pursue this project. This book is not a complete and accurate record of all one-room schools in Iowa. It is an attempt to develop a comprehensive statewide report that I hope will lead to a better understanding of the important role one-room schools have played in Iowa's history and heritage.

About the Editor

The idea for this book was developed by William L. Sherman, public relations specialist for the Iowa State Education Association (ISEA). Sherman became interested in one-room schools as work was completed on the book he edited in 1996, *Tributes to Iowa Teachers.* Preliminary research revealed no current information was available on the number of one-room schools that remained in the state. So he set about the task of compiling this data from contacts in each county. He recruited William Dreier, Nancy Barry, Erik Eriksen and others to share their knowledge about one-room schools; and collected the photographs and artwork that appear in this book.

Sherman has worked for the ISEA in various publication and public relations capacities since 1964. He earned two degrees from the University of Iowa and has taken additional graduate work at Drake University and Iowa State University. He was accredited by the Public Relations Society of America in 1993.

One-Room School Video Available

If you are looking for additional information about Iowa's one-room schools, consider ordering a new video—*The Legacy of the One-Room School.* This video was developed from a slide-tape presentation produced by Robert Hardman for the Cedar Falls Historical Society. Hardman is professor of education and director of Information Technology Services/Training at the University of Northern Iowa.

The video describes the program presented in one-room schools at the turn of the century. Authentic visuals obtained from various Iowa schools are used to illustrate the 23-minute program. The video would be a valuable program resource for students planning to visit a country school, and for adults who want to reminisce about country school life.

The cost of the video is $25. This includes shipping charges. *The Legacy of the One-Room School* can be ordered by sending a check made payable to Iowa State Education Association to: ISEA Public Relations Office, 4025 Tonawanda Drive, Des Moines, Iowa 50312. Please include a complete street address and name with the order.

Table of Contents

Preface

Iowa's one-room schools. They were landmarks of learning. And the teachers who taught in them made Iowa a leader in learning. That's the legacy of the one-room school. And it's a legacy that continues to impact teachers and students in Iowa schools today.

The idea for a book about Iowa's one-room schools originated during Iowa's sesquicentennial observance. ISEA developed a book for that occasion entitled *Tributes to Iowa Teachers*. In that publication two of the contributors wrote about their experiences with a teacher in a one-room country school. Research that followed revealed a revival in interest around Iowa in preserving Iowa's one-room schools. Many counties undertook sesquicentennial projects that related to one-room schools. Further research revealed little current information about the status of one-room schools in Iowa. No one had any idea how many of these schools were still in existence.

So in November of 1996, following the end of one publishing project, another was started. Following discussions with several individuals, letters were sent to local and county historical societies asking for help in identifying the number of one-room schools that remained in the county and the ways those schools were being used. That request for information led to identification of a group of volunteers who made this book possible.

These are the goals we established for this publication:

1. Provide a historical overview of the growth and development of one-room schools in Iowa to help more people better understand the contributions made by these schools and the teachers who taught in them. William Dreier, professor emeritus at the University of Northern Iowa, provides this historical overview.

2. Describe how the teaching and learning in one-room schools have influenced education taking place in Iowa schools today. Nancy Barry, a Luther College faculty member whose research has involved interviews with former one-room school teachers and former one-room school students, provides several ideas on this topic.

3. Create a county-by-county summary that includes information about the number of one-room schools standing and the ways those buildings are currently being used.

4. Produce a comprehensive photographic record of Iowa country schools past and present.

The cover was designed to establish the tone for the book. We tried to create a visual that reflects both the contents of the book and the dynamics of the country school movement in Iowa today.

Grant Wood's *Arbor Day* painting is perhaps the most recognizable image created of an Iowa country school. This school, which was once located near Koings Mark not far from Cedar Rapids, no longer stands. But the one-room school that Grant Wood attended—Antioch—has been preserved as a museum by the Anamosa Paint 'n Pallette Club. This painting reinforces our nostalgic view of country schools and simpler times.

The photograph of the restored country school now located on the school grounds at Rowley captures the rebirth of the country school preservation movement that is taking place at rural and urban locations throughout Iowa. This picture was taken by Dave Gosch, a reporter/photographer for the *Cedar Rapids Gazette* at dedication ceremonies September 12, 1996.

Together the painting and photograph reflect the dynamics of the one-room school influence. They illustrate the idyllic view of the past and the youthful potential for our future.

As an outgrowth of this book, ISEA obtained a REAP/Historical Resource Development Grant from the Sate Historical Society of Iowa to develop a group nomination to place additional country schools on the National Register of Historic Places. Fewer than twenty Iowa school building are currently listed. Many more deserve this recognition.

William L. Sherman, APR
Public Relations Specialist
Iowa State Education Association
4025 Tonawanda Drive
Des Moines, Iowa 50312
Phone: 515-279-9711

Walnut Grove School, Scott County

Revisiting Iowa's One-Room Schools

They're all over Iowa, no more
than two miles apart, these one-room museums
of memories: mounted pictures
of Washington and Lincoln,
the American flag standing in the corner
like a close friend to the globe,
a black, silver-rimmed potbellied stove
down its own aisle in the center
of the world, warming a hickory stick
across the teacher's desk,
a big red apple, two hand bells, books
and, next to the piano,
waiting on a four-legged stool,
a dunce's cap. Facing the teacher
sits the recitation bench
where crowded students spoke
their golden words. You can still read
Matt's ditty to Mary, the one
he carved on his desk five rows back,
just below the inkwell
where he dipped Peggy's pigtails
like paintbrushes
into the bottle out of respect
for penmanship, for art,
and for the right effect.

Miss Hirl's lessons covered
the alphabet, the three Rs,
Iowa history, and a poem on the board
to memorize. "Remember these lines,"
she told her students before summer
break. In seconds, only
a schoolhouse remained
in the clearing. Suzy waited
for her dad's trail
of dust, white
as pounded erasure
chalk. His pickup's coming
over the hill while in his mind,
straight as a corn row, ran the order
for consolidation. She waved
to her teacher who beamed
with students' progress
in orthography, music, and sums,
while carpenters in town
gather their tools
and check their plans
to start another lesson.

—Dick Stahl, English teacher,
Davenport Central High School

Remembering
Iowa's Country Schools

P. Buckley Moss
School Picnic
Living History Farms, Polk County

A Brief History of Iowa's One-Room Schools

William H. Dreier
Professor of Education, Emeritus
University of Northern Iowa

The most common picture of the Iowa country school is a white wood-frame building sitting alone on about one acre of land, beside a dirt road, surrounded by a fence with fields or timberland beyond. There were many names given to this one-teacher school and normally one-room school. It was referred to as the rural school, the common school, a primary school, a nongraded or an ungraded school, the county superintendent's school, the district school, the township school, or the public school. In Iowa it was common to call these schools "country schools," but those who attended them generally identified them by their township number—Jackson #5, Honey Creek #2, Bennington #4.

The country school did not begin in Iowa but came along with the early settlers from the eastern regions of the United States. While rural schools were found in other countries, for most the start of the country school can be attributed to Thomas Jefferson. In 1779, Jefferson, then a member of the General Assembly of the Commonwealth of Virginia, introduced a "Bill for the More General Diffusion of Knowledge." It provided for three Aldermen to be chosen from each county. They were responsible for dividing the county to make up schools that would teach "...reading, writing and common arithmetick, and the books used shall be such as will be at the same time make them acquainted with Graecian, Roman, English and American history." Education was to be free for three years and at private expense thereafter.

Jefferson's ideas were implemented in his authorship of the Northwest Ordinance of 1785 which organized newly acquired territory north of the Ohio River west to the Mississippi River. Six-mile by six-mile townships were surveyed and each of the 36-square-mile sections were numbered for identification. The Contintental Congress provided that section 16 of every township would be reserved for the maintenance of public schools. In the rules on government, the Northwest Ordinance of 1787 included this succinct phrase: "Religion, morality, and knowledge being necessary for good government and the happiness of mankind, schools and means of educa-

tion shall forever be encouraged" (184 Wall 1978). These principles were extended to the Louisiana Purchase territory from which Iowa became a state in 1846.

The first school in Iowa was a country school located near the Mississippi River where it was joined by the Des Moines River from the west. A Dr. Galland founded a settlement (first called Nashville, then Galland) in the Half-Breed Tract and established a private, subscription school in 1830. Mr. Berryman Jennings, a Kentuckian, was employed by Galland as the teacher. (335 Guide 1986) Mrs. Rebecca Farmer's school, established in 1834 in Fort Madison, also in Lee County, was the second school and there were several other similar schools prior to 1836. Still, when Robert Lucas arrived on the scene to be first governor of the Iowa Territory that year, he was dismayed to find a lack of public schools in the territory (185 Wall 1978).

A flavor of these early schools may be found in the diary of Arizona Perkins. She was born in Vermont in 1826 and came west with 26 trained teachers, traveling by stage coach, boat and train. Perkins first went to Fort Des Moines, a town of 3000, to start a subscription school. In November, 1850, she wrote: "I found things here very different from my expectations with regard to the wants of the people. Mrs. Bird has a new schoolhouse just completed, and the only one in town, and a school of about 40 children. Of this I was totally ignorant until since I came here. There is a district school three months in the year, usually in the winter, and one of the trustees commenced it at the Court House, but the other two objecting to his terms, and, determined to have a school on a cheap scale, hired another man, and turned Mr. G. out of the house" (127 Kaufman 1984). Later in the month she began a school in a church with nine scholars and on December 21, 1850, reported the number was 24. This from her diary for February 8, 1851: "Closed my term yesterday. Can't say yet whether I shall be able to clear all expenses or not. Expect when I get what clothes worn out that I bro't with me I shall be obliged to wear a blanket, for all things are so dear here that

I never can make enough to clothed me decently. Paid out my last dime the other day for postage of the letter I sent to S. 'The earth is the Lord's and the fullness thereof" (127 Kaufman 1984).

The first Territorial Assembly established a system of common schools in 1839. These were the subscription, or rate schools, meaning parents had to pay tuition. It was not until 1858 that the common schools were converted into free schools. The change was greatly influenced by a recommendation of Horace Mann, the first state superintendent of schools (Massachusetts) in the nation and the dominant influence on public education. He was asked to head a commission in 1858 to study and report on Iowa's educational needs. Much of this report was embodied in Iowa's second constitution and continued, in modified form, until today. While his idea of a state Board of Education was rejected, for fear of arbitrary centralized authority, the concept of using property tax to fund the schools and the longer school year were accepted. The locally funded school district, under local control, would remain the basis of Iowa's educational system for nearly a century.

During the early years of statehood, there were town independent districts and township districts for the rural areas. The townships were allowed to create nine sub-districts that would remain under the authority of the township Board of Education. But the demand to have total local control and to have an independent district similar to the towns led to change in 1872 by the General Assembly. Now a township could have up to nine independent districts, made up of four contiguous sections, each with its own three-member board. Within a few years, most townships voted to accept this alternative, increasing the number of school districts dramatically. But this did not solve all the problems.

Location remained a point of contention. Normally the school was situated at the center of the four sections of the district. But the distribution of the scholars, or the personal preferences of a dominant family, might lead to the relocation of the school building. This was possible in the 19th century when schools were built on skids and could be moved by a team of horses. U. C. Miller of Orange Township related that he had attended school in the same building but in three different locations (30 Snavely 1967).

Everyone had access to a school, but what was the quality of the education? In the last quarter of the 19th century, many observers saw it barely adequate. Hamlin Garland remembered his experience in *Boy's Life on the Prairie:* "The Schoolhouse stood a mile away on the prairie with not even a fence to shield it from the blast ... painted a glaring white on the outside and a drab within... this bare building on the naked prairie seemed a poor place indeed" (186 Wall 1978). Historian Joseph Wall summarized this way: "Indeed, it was a poor place, yet it provided the only education that hundreds of thousands of Iowans were ever to receive. Dependent almost entirely upon local property tax levies for support, the rural school districts had only the barest of sustenance, hardly enough to put up adequate buildings, provide the minimum furnishings, and hire as teachers young girls who themselves had only an eighth-grade education, for whatever each individual teacher

Cherokee County, circa 1900.

4

was able to collect from the parents of her pupils. As late as 1896, the average length of attendance for the country school pupil was a little less than two months per year..." (186 Wall 1978).

The rural school was an integral part of a community. It served the need for formal education, was the voting center, a place of entertainment and a source of news. The standard two-mile by two-mile rural independent school district included four sections. At the turn of the century, with farms often no larger than 40 acres, a section could have five families, meaning a school would serve as many as twenty families. Farm families were large, to meet the labor demands, and it was not unusual for one family to send as many as ten children to the one-room school for an education.

The need for country schools was never hard to document and was accepted by the people of Iowa who responded by building and staffing thousands of schools. The largest number in Iowa was in 1901 when there were 12,623 one-room schools (Biennial Report). That year the state could boast of having the greatest number in the nation. By 1932-33 there were still 9,279 one-room schools in operation, but the number was starting to decline. The number of farms per section was smaller and the size of the families were not as large. By 1910, there were 3,018 schools that had less than ten students and ten schools had only one student (186 Wall 1978).

Another factor in the reduction of rural schools was consolidation. Declining enrollment, the desire to improve educational opportunity, and the intent to reduce costs led some independent districts to consolidate. In some areas, like Buffalo Township in Winnebago County in 1895, the area voted to form a Town Independent District around Buffalo Center village. Eventually all the districts closed and students were taken to Buffalo Center in horse-drawn hacks. In this action they became the first Consolidated School District west of the Mississippi River (1 Dreier 1995).

Other consolidations followed, though slowly. The second was at Terrill in Dickinson County in 1901; the third at Marathon, Pocahontas County, 1902; and the fourth in Lake Township, Clay County in 1903 (331 Sage 1974 and 3 Campbell 1921).

The pace quickened with new state legislation in 1906 and 1910 to encourage change. Some districts close to larger cities, like Orange Township in Black Hawk County, voted to consolidate and build a high school rather than send their children to Waterloo. Consolidation continued through 1921. By then, 439 consolidated districts had been creat-

ed with only the counties of Ida, Lyon, Howard, and Winneshiek not having one (1 Campbell 1921). About 75 percent of the area of the state continued with their one-room, one-teacher systems.

The changes were substantial. Students went from one-room schools with one teacher to multi-room buildings and many teachers, from ungraded to graded systems, from being in the familar environment of the country to the new atmosphere of the village or town, from little or no opportunity to work beyond eighth grade to the chance for a high school diploma, and from a walk-in school for children to a bussed-in school for children and youth. The Orange Township situation was a reflection of the problems. The teachers in Orange Township suggested a consolidation plan used in Indiana. A vote to consolidate nine schools was taken in 1914 and failed, three to one. The discussion continued among the farmers and some decided to travel to Indiana to see for themselves. In 1915 another vote was taken and the idea was accepted, three to one. A consolidated district of 40 sections was created, a school board elected, and a bond levy of $55,000 approved to build an elementary/secondary grade building.

When the new building was opened in September 1916, all the one-room school buildings were sold or abandoned and the students transported to the new central building. Initially there were some problems: "The line of horse-drawn hacks moved up the muddy road where 200 or more children were unloaded and brought together into one school system for the first time. The children of each district carried with them the prejudices toward children in the other districts." But these were soon resolved by the staff of a superintendent, principal and five teachers (78 Snavely 1967). Orange Township was an exception, however, for most country districts did not combine to create a high school or to establish some equity among township schools. For most farmers, consolidation was a four-letter word that brought the specter of loss of local control and the threat of higher property taxes.

The years between 1922 and 1953 saw little change in the number of school districts. As farm commodity prices fell in the 1920s and remained low in the 1930s, there was little incentive to raise property taxes to build new schools for a reorganized system. It was cheaper to maintain the elementary system in the country school and then pay the tuition to the nearby town or consolidated school for those who wanted to continue their education. Some country schools with low enrollments began to pay tuition to send their students to neighboring districts rather than have the expense of operating a nearly empty building. But during these years the number of organized districts did not change dramatically, only dropping from 4,639 in 1922 to 4,558 in 1953. The fear of loss of local control and higher property taxes, plus the belief that country schools provided an adequate education, led the list of reasons to maintain the status quo.

Change was in the air, however, and in the years after World War II, the role of one-room schools became a major political and educational issue in the state. Class size and quality of education were reasons for many to advocate the forced consolidation of country school districts. Comments by teacher Jean Porter describe what was happening:

"It was the school year 1942 to 1943. I taught the year before in a consolidated school, before I was married. This school was in Gibson and I taught kindergarten, first and second grades. I didn't know if it was moving up, down or sideways when I moved from one school to another because I had never attended country school.... I had six grades [in the new school]. Two classes had just one student each; there were just 12 students in all.... We had a nice furnace in the basement. The kids roller skated down there. The hardest thing to do to change to Country School was the classes that had just one child. It was awfully hard to motivate that one child. That was the weak link in Country Schools...." (118 Cedar 1995).

Across the state the country school numbers were declining. In 1955-56, Iowa had 808 high school districts (town and consolidated) and 3,334 non-high school districts (township and rural independent) (49 Great 1968). World War II was

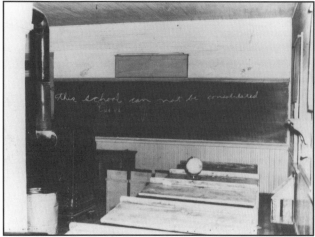

Madison #1, near Truro, 1945.

over, land values had been increasing for several years, and farms were growing in size. At the same time, the number of farmers had been declining by 10 percent per decade for some time, reducing the available school population. In addition, many farm-to-market roads were surfaced, making it easier for rural students to attend town schools. During this period school enrollments were increasing in nearly every community with a census count of at least 500 people. As the junior and senior high population grew, there was a demand for new schools. These factors converged in the early 1950s to bring change to the state's educational system.

The "great school change" was a contentious and difficult time. In 1945 the state had mandated that each County Board of Education prepare a plan that would allow a realignment of country schools into natural neighborhoods. This resulted in a few new consolidations. In 1947, the General Assembly called for a halt in all reorganization to allow more extensive study by the County Boards on consolidation. The moritorium ended in 1953 when Iowa school law was changed to require each of the non-high school districts to join with a high school unit by 1962. The new districts would have at least 300 students, kindergarten through grade 12. The new community school district would also decide whether it would continue to use the one-room schools in the joining districts or close them. In 1955, legislation was passed that would close all country schools as of June 1, 1966. The result was 50 new community school districts being formed in 1954. The year that brought the largest number of consolidated districts was 1958-59 when 829 districts merged to form 102 new school units (22-3 Dreier 1967). All the new districts had to transport children to the schools, making the yellow school bus the most conspicuous vehicle on Iowa county roads (188 Wall 1978).

The consolidation movement of the 1950s did not solve the problem. As rural areas continued to be depopulated, the small school districts found it difficult to survive. Over the next 40 years consolidated schools, like the one-room schools before them, had to adapt. The Buffalo Center Consolidated School story was typical of the process. It had been created in 1897 by combining 36 sections. In November 1953 voters approved a plan of reorganization. On July 1, 1954, Buffalo Township Consolidated School District became part of the Buffalo Center Community School District. They were joined by four one-room school units in Winnebago County and part of a fifth school unit in Kossuth County. In 1978 the district joined with Rake Community School District. In 1992 Buffalo Center-Rake joined with the Lakota Consolidated School. In 1995 the North Iowa Community School District was created when Buffalo Center-Rake-Lakota voted to join Thompson Community School. The new districts included 315 sections of land (5 Dreier 1995).

There continued to be resistance in some areas to joining a high school district. In 1962, the General Assembly passed legislation that would allow the state to assign any unattached district to a high school district not done voluntarily by 1967. By 1966 there were only 46 non-high school districts and by the deadline of 1967, only 19 districts were remained to be assigned.

Not all country schools were closed in 1967. The Iowa Code provided for "Schools Operated by Exempt Religious Groups" to operate as approved private schools. In 1996-97 there were 37 such schools in 12 counties with 895 children enrolled. The Old Order Amish operate 29; the Mennonite five; and the Beechy Amish, New Order Amish, and Bretheran each have one school. In addition to these private schools, there are six Amish schools in northeast Iowa which are operated by public schools, the Jesup and Wapsie Valley School Districts (Stokes 1996).

The country school contributed to the Iowa educational system in many ways. It was, first and foremost, the primary school system from 1830-1945 for most Iowans. It produced quality people, some of whom, like Norman Borlaug, became international figures and others, like Jessie Field Shambaugh, were active at the state level. But whether farmers or bankers, homemakers or educators, the country school provided the educational base which served its students well throughout their lives.

There were other contributions as well. The country school fulfilled Jefferson's dream for an educated common citizenry without which democracy would not be able to thrive. For years McGuffy's Readers taught civic responsibility, moral values, and religious commitment. The schools reduced illiteracy in Iowa to the lowest level in the nation by 1890, a position the state was to hold for years to come. However, Historian Joseph Wall suggested this was not all good, for it allowed a degree of complacency and slowed educational reform (187 Wall 1978).

Indirectly the schools also helped Americanize the immigrants who came to Iowa. Prior to 1900 most were farm workers whose children attended one-room schools and who not only learned English and American customs there, but also brought these back home for their parents. Many lessons were taught a second time at a kitchen table after the dinner dishes had been washed and put away in the evening.

The country school was and continues to be a major factor in the preservation and growth of small groups of people with a life-style based on deep religious conviction. The Amish in Iowa are able to maintain their traditions and values in large part because their children attend their own schools.

The rural school districts provided "hands on" political experience. Iowa, as did many other states, began local government with the township. Township trustees collected poll tax (mainly for local road use), decided on local disputes over property lines, closed and improved roads, selected local voting sites, and provided local political leadership. Likewise, the locally elected school board members had to deal with the concerns of the district as well as

Cerro Gordo County, 1911　　　　　　　*©Concord Camera Corp.*

7

increasingly deal with county and state educational officials.

The one-room school was the starting point for many educators. Homer Seerley, president of Iowa State Teachers College in Cedar Falls for 50 years, credited his early one-room school experiences in forming his future professional life. After two years in engineering at the University of Iowa, he taught in a rural school and found it so rewarding that he left engineering and made education his career (91 Lang 1990).

Not all country school experiences were positive. Many teachers found the schools dominated by one family which tried to run the school. Others found the directors too tight-fisted, unwilling to pay fair salaries or buy materials. Still others tried to use their family ties to the area to get teaching jobs, sometimes without the proper qualifications. These problems drove many qualified teachers from the country schools to positions in towns and cities. However, many others found the one-room schoolhouse a challenging and rewarding job and spent most, if not all, of their careers in one school.

Country schools provided new opportunities for women to develop a professional career and influence the values of a community. In 1876 the Iowa State Normal School (now the University of Northern Iowa) made an important contribution in preparing both women and men for the teaching profession. Women not only brought their educational skills to rural areas, they also conveyed their broader view of the world to communities that were often isolated and closed to change. When a teacher married a local man, that experience was extended to a new family and to the neighborhood.

Student teachers learned the practical side of education in one-room schools. Between 1883 and the 1950s, Iowa State Normal School and other colleges placed students there to gain experience. The student teachers encountered a wide range of grade levels and classroom situations. The classroom teacher and students benefited from the additional help. One country school closed and transferred its students to the Model School (later Price Laboratory School) at Iowa State Normal School (106 Hart 1951).

For those who attended one-room schools, there were many personal benefits. The school population was small so there was individual attention, either from the teacher or from an older student. To a certain extent, students were allowed to advance at their own pace. There was a sense of carefreeness and security among the children as everyone knew each other. Finally, the schools provided an identity and a tradition. To have attended Bennington #3 meant you would be bonded to those classmates for the rest of your life and the memories you shared would be the fondest ones you might have.

Country schools were at the core of the Iowa experience in the 19th and first half of the 20th century. Perhaps as many as 75 percent of the population were educated there. Their social and cultural perspectives were shaped in the schools. Graduates credited their success to the values and skills they learned there. One-room schools were the landmarks that gave direction to Iowa's growth and development.

Herbert Quick School, Grundy Center

An Iowa Country School Chronology

1830	First school formed in future state of Iowa in Lee County.
1846	Iowa becomes a state with 30 organized counties and a constitution that says "the General Assembly shall provide for a system of common schools."
1857	Iowa adopts new constitution and "from that time on a permanent and prosperous school system has been developing" (277 Sabin 1900).
1858	Iowa makes the township the unit for common schools and provides for the town independent district for common schooling, including education of grammar grades and high school.
1872	Rural Independent School Districts created when Township residents voted to make each sub-district independent (2 Ghan 1996).
1876	Iowa State Normal School at Cedar Falls established for the support of the Common Schools.
1896	United States establishes Rural Free Delivery in Iowa, increasing interest in good country roads which facilitates movement of students as well.
1897	Iowa grants funds for school transportation which marks the start of closing of one-room township schools. First Consolidated School District established at Buffalo Center in Winnebago County.
1901	The number of one-room schools in Iowa peaks with 12,623 in operation, more than any other state.
1902	Iowa requires all children ages 7 to 14 to attend school.
1921	Iowa has 439 consolidated school districts in 94 of 99 counties.
1932	Iowa has 9,279 one-room schools. Only Illinois has more with 10,041.
1946	End of high school normal training courses for new teachers in Iowa.
1952	All new teachers in Iowa must have at least two years of appropriate education for certification.
1953	The law forming Community School Districts to include all the non-high school districts closes most country schools that were one-room districts.
1958	There are 102 new Community School Districts formed to meet the requirements of State rules.
1960	After this year all new teachers certified in Iowa required to have a B.A. Degree.
1965	*The Des Moines Register* photograph of Amish students running into a cornfield leads to legislative passage of a law allowing religious groups to operate their own schools. That law remains in 1998.
1997	Research conducted by the Iowa State Education Association reveals that more than 2,800 former one-room schools remain in existence in Iowa. More than 180 of these schools have been preserved as museums open for visitors.
1998	Nearly 40 one-room schools are being used by religious groups to provide instruction to approximately 1,000 children.

Bibliography

Biennial Report of the Iowa Superintendent of Public Instruction. Des Moines, 1896, 1901, 1903.

Campbell, Macy. *Growth of Consolidated Schools in Iowa.* Cedar Falls: Bulletin of the Iowa State Teachers College, Vol. XXII, No. 3, 1921. 16pp.

Cedar Falls Historical Society. Oral Histories - Teachers and Pupils of One-Room Schools. Cedar Falls: Cedar Falls Historical Society, 1993-94. 268pp.

Dreier, William H. *The Community School District in Iowa.* Cedar Falls: University of Northern Iowa, Extension Service, 1967. 98pp.

_____. *One-Room Schools Preserved as Museums in Iowa.* Cedar Falls: University of Northern Iowa, 1990, 1993, 1996. 5pp.

_____ and Pilgrim, Ronald. "100 Years of Change for Better Schools." Report to the 87th National Rural Education Conference, October 8, 1996. 16pp.

Fuller, Wayne. *The Old Country School. The Story of Rural Education in the Middle West.* Chicago: University of Chicago Press, 1982. 302pp.

Ghan, Guy W. List of Current Reorganization Activities. Des Moines: Department of Education, Reorganization Series XIX, July 1, 1996. 16pp.

Guilliford, Andrew. *America's Country Schools.* Boulder: University Press of Colorado, 1996. 3rd Edition. 294pp.

Hart, Irving H. *The First Fifty Years.* Cedar Falls: Iowa State Teachers College, 1951. 106pp.

Kaufman, Polly Welts. *Women Teachers on the Frontier.* New Haven: Yale University Press, 1984. 27opp.

Lang, William C. *A Century of Leadership and Service. A Centennial History of the University of Northern Iowa. Volume I.* Cedar Falls: UNI Foundation, 1990. 563pp.

_____ and Pendergraft, Darrell. *A Century of Leadership and Service. A Centennial History of the University of Northern Iowa. Volume II.* Cedar Falls: UNI Foundation, 1995. 547pp.

Morgan, Barton and Lancelot, W.H. *A Possible Intermediate Step in the Reorganization of Rural Education in Iowa.* Ames: Iowa State University, Research Bulletin No. 200, June, 1936.

Riley, Glenda. *Cities on the Cedar. A Portrait of Cedar Falls, Waterloo and Black Hawk County.* Parkersburg: Mid-Prairie Books, 1988. 124pp.

Sabin, Henry and Sabin, Edward. *The Making of Iowa.* New York: A. Flannagan Co., 1900,1916. 284pp.

Snavely, Ida B. *Orange Township Lore Pieced into Patchwork.* Waterloo: Pioneer Advertiser, 1967. 100pp.

Stokes, Clifford H. Iowa Department of Education, Exempt School Consultant. Telephone call 12/11/96 and letter 12/14/96.

Tyack, David B. (Editor). *Turning Points in American Educational History.* Waltham, MA: Blaisdell Publishing, 1967. 488pp.

Wall, Joseph F. *Iowa. A Bicentennial History.* New York: W. W. Norton, 1978. 212pp.

Works Progress Administration. *WPA Guide to 1930s Iowa.* Ames: Iowa State University Press, 1986. 583pp.

Architectural Styles for Iowa's One-Room Schools

by Steve Johnson
Decorah

The rural schoolhouse survey of Winneshiek County uncovered 18 architectural styles. These styles, which were common throughout Iowa and the upper Midwest, are illustrated at the end of this article.

By far the most common roof style was the gable roof. The earliest schools were patterned after the homes in the communities and were made of logs. The locations of the door(s) and chimney, as well as the presence of a bell tower, allowed for many variations of the gable roof schoolhouse. Between 1900 and 1920, some schools were built with a clipped gable roof. The hip and hip-with-ridge roof styles appeared around the 1920s. Apparently, the public still preferred the traditional rectangular-shaped schoolhouse, as only a few of the hip schools were constructed.

The window arrangement for the early rural schoolhouses had two to four sets of windows on opposing walls used for cross lighting. By the early 1920s, the state superintendent's office had issued new standards which endorsed the use of a bank of windows on only one elevation. It had been determined that cross lighting was harmful to pupils' eyes.

The Bungalow-style schools appeared in Iowa around 1920. Most of these schoolhouses incorporated the hip or hip-with-ridge roof design. Typically, these schools had column supports for a porch or an attic overhang.

The last rural schools were built in the late 1940s with a new style of architecture called the "International." With many rural school districts beginning to consolidate, these structures tend to be limited in number. These schools were similar in their cube-like form, characterized by flat roof, the avoidance of applied surface decoration, and an emphasis on volume or space enclosed by thin planes and surfaces. They were built of cement-block walls and poured concrete basements, and included automatic oil furnaces, indoor toilets, electric lights, and modern kitchens.

The common roof arrangement did not include a bell tower. Most schools utilized the smaller hand-held bell to call the pupils in from recess.

Only about 12 percent of the schoolhouses in Winneshiek County had a bell tower. Their locations would either be above the entry on the gable peak, situated along the interior partition wall, or on an addition to the entry area.

Most, if not all, early schoolhouses were built without basements. By the turn of the century, communities were changing from wood or coal stoves to a furnace system. This created a need for a basement to hold the furnace. Unfortunately, many of the school basements built were not structurally sound, and in their later years, settled unevenly causing much damage and expense to repair the buildings. Beginning with the Bungalow-style schoolhouse, these structures had internal accesses to their basements, which housed the furnaces and provided an alternative recreational area to the playground.

The chimneys for schoolhouses typically were located on the peak of the roof. Many were on the opposing wall from the entry. If the schoolhouse had a front hallway or cloakroom, the stove for the school was located on the interior wall in the main room. This would allow the stovepipe to run along the length of the ceiling to a chimney on the far wall. Over the course of time, the location of the chimney could change when a furnace was installed to replace the stove. It appears that the earlier schools had internal stepped brick chimneys, while later ones originated in the basement or ground level of the school.

Although common in the northeastern United States, the two-door entry was an unusual style in northeast Iowa. Used in the early days of rural school construction, records indicated that one door was used by boys and the other by the girls. Since many of the early schools were first held in pioneer homes before the community could build a schoolhouse, the concept of having two entry doors may not have been familiar to them.

The earliest schools did not have a cloakroom. A number of schools in the 1860s to 1870s added small shed additions which served as their cloakroom. By 1890, schools were being constructed with an internal entry hall leading into the main classroom. Many schools had the internal basement steps located in the cloakroom.

The basic floor plan for the majority of the rural schoolhouses was rectangular in form. In the early school days this was due to the introduction of the front hallway leading into the classroom. The later schools needed additional floor space for bathrooms, coat rooms, and kitchens.

The allowance for light may have played a key role in determining the width of the structure. From measurements, it appears that the formula was consistently in the range of 18- to 24-foot widths and 28- to 32-foot lengths for the schools up to the 1920s. The Bungalow-style schoolhouse, with its hip-with-ridge roof, changed the design to a less rectangular shape. The limited existence of the hip roof structures supports the theory that the preference was for a rectangular building. The ridge portion of the hip roof provided the additional lengths needed for rectangular schools.

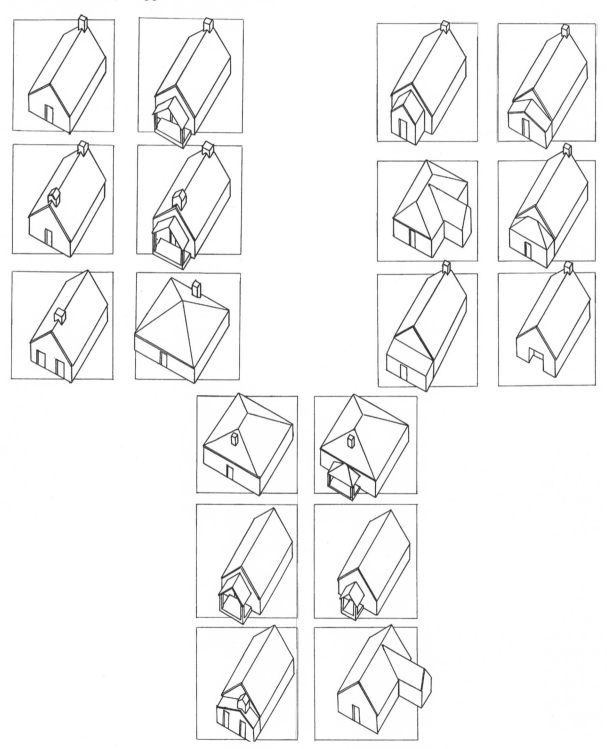

12

The Continuing Influence of One-Room Schools

by Nancy K. Barry
Associate Professor of English, Luther College

With their distinctive architecture and regular placement, one-room schools have woven their way into the historical landscape of Iowa—a visible reminder that our first citizens decided to make intellectual growth as central to their economy as crops and cows.

There is a mystique to these buildings, at least to someone like me—an adult who early on in her life caught the fever for learning and has since spent every year from autumn to May either as a student or teacher. I came to the Iowa landscape late in my schooling years, after the apprenticeship of a Master's and Ph.D. degree. Then the freedom from academic requirements gave me the space and time to think about learning.

For several summers, I worked as an instructor in the Iowa Writing Project, a team of teachers committed to the principles of active learning for students in grades K-12, particularly in terms of their intellectual growth as writers and readers. These summer institutes became seed-beds for my continuing study of how and why classrooms work to foster real learning in students. Invariably, one of the participating teachers would remind me that much of what I would describe as "cutting edge" pedagogy had in fact its origin in the practice and routines of one-room country schools.

Fayette County

"This isn't so new," one language arts teacher commented after we had discussed the importance of student writers using an extended circle of peers as an audience for their early drafts. "When I went to country school, we did this type of thing all the time. In fact, everything you're describing about cooperative learning we did first-hand in our school, all the time. There were only 14 of us, but that teacher had us working all the time—older to younger. Whatever you learned, you ended up teaching to another child who hadn't caught on yet. Country schools were the most cooperative classrooms ever designed."

When that workshop was over, my driving tour took me past several remnants of one-room schools—some dilapidated and forlorn, some refurbished into museums or homes. I found myself inevitably drawn to these buildings as symbols for what was gained and lost in our path toward modernizing our schools. As if in wandering up to the door and peering through the windows, I could take an imaginative journey into what it meant for teachers to work in those classrooms, and for children to grow older, if not smarter and wiser, in the string of chairs that marked their age and grade. In my travels around the state as a writing teacher and lecturer for the Iowa Humanities Board, I began to listen more closely for the stories and memories of those who had taught or learned in these one-room school houses and I realized quite quickly that—despite their sometimes primitive or isolated conditions—these schools promoted a sense of learning and citizenship that we would do well to rediscover in our post-modern age.

I don't intend to romanticize the schools, to paint them with the veneer of Norman Rockwell and make them seem tirelessly quaint or heroic. Many of the schools struggled not just for sufficient heat, but books as well. Teachers could find themselves in a perpetual battle with a community's tight-fisted grasp of funds, and indeed had to prove their ability in the school not just as a teacher, but as maintenance worker or nurse as well. These schools were isolated, and particularly lonely for teachers who worked in virtual isolation in the building. Imagine being 16, 18, or perhaps 20 years old, with merely a high school or academy degree tucked into your suitcase. Your first job is a one-room school with 20 children, ranging in age from 6 to 17. No "in-service" days to get you started; no statewide lesson plans to provide guidance; no teacher down the hall with more experience to mentor or coach. If a life-threatening emergency appeared, your help was only as quick as the best runner in the class. For women, being a country school teacher was as much a way of life as it was a profession. Communities provided room and board. The surest way to be released from your contract was to get married.

For students, the experience could foster more fear than curiosity. Then, as now, children were capable of bullying one another, and one room doesn't leave much space for neutral territories. Teachers have gladly forsaken many dim-sighted strategies in that learning environment: rote memorization, with little or no regard for the context or purpose of what was being spoken aloud; recitation as the sole means of gauging intelligence or aptitude; sentence parsing used not just as the backbone, but the whole body of language instruction. So we should all be wary of inviting that age back wholesale—either for its culture or pedagogy. Rather, it seems wiser to study the heritage and history of these classrooms as a way of identifying those practices that helped transform the minds and lives of students. The best way to find those is by using a decidedly subjective assessment instrument: simply asking both students and teachers "what worked?"

Their answers, given either in published journals on Iowa history or in shared conversation among fellow teachers, prove that one-room schools had a profound effect on their sense of audience, language, and shared responsibility for learning. For each of these items, I could use a phrase from our current educational jargon, such as "rhetorical context," "whole language," "cooperative learning," or "individualized instruction." That one-room schools were filled with such practices years before the teaching profession codified them into terms is a testimony to the ingenuity and grace of those teachers. It is a reminder to all of us that life-long learning depends more on the quality of interaction between teacher and student, as well as student and classmate. At their core, one-room schoolhouses were structural reinforcements of a fundamental idea about public education: it is a shared, not solitary venture. It is only as strong as the cooperative links formed among teachers, students, and community.

To many of the students who learned in these schools, the learning perhaps felt more coercive than it did cooperative. The presence of so many of one's neighbors, both older and younger, lent an urgency to one's work. A woman who grew up near Coin, Iowa, remembers the rigor of having to read and recite in front of a room filled with listening ears. She noted: "The members of the class made

Fayette County

corrections, if any, on the performance, and we were meticulous in our criticism of such errors as mispronouncing a word, or hesitating, or using the wrong inflection."

For thousands of children in one-room schools, the concept of "audience" was never imaginary. These learners had a vested interest in the performance and mastery of one another, and thus worked daily in an environment in which learning and "assessment" were shared activities. As teachers, we traded in the routine of such performances for solitary, individualized workbooks and paper drill sheets. We made the process of writing, reading, or learning a solely private matter between the student, the pencil, and the teacher.

What was lost was the most fundamental thing anyone who is learning to communicate needs to know: how does this sound to an audience of real people? The one-room schoolhouse, with its use of recitation and reading aloud, made "performers" out of all students, and created an environment for students to hear and respond to the voices of their peers.

This oral tradition in the one-room schools made them a far better environment to teach and absorb the musical dimensions of language, particularly through poetry or song. One former student remembers keenly how even something as simple as the daily roll call would evoke a stanza of poetry or Biblical verse as a way of saying "I'm here." Poetry—particularly ballads and short lyrics—was a staple of country schools because it was presented as language to be heard. Its meaning depended both on the speaker's ability to make the music felt in the sense of the line, but also on the shared experience of all those listening.

In addition to the shared texts of familiar poems, many students recall how much singing was done in those rooms. "Singing was a way to calm us down and get us ready for study," one woman recalls. In her remembrance we can all hear a gentle reminder that anyone approaching the space and the time for intellectual work needs to "calm down," to gear the mind toward contemplation and concentration. Singing—especially in a group—is one way of making the disparate energy of so many separate people come together, and creates both a literal and metaphorical harmony.

Fayette County

Perhaps the modern counterpart to such an activity is "Channel One," the piped-in video segments that begin the school days of many children. In the difference between these two activities we can see everything about what has been won and lost in our classrooms. Next to images of Tianenmen Square, a classroom full of students singing a ballad from the Civil War probably seems like pretty dull stuff. But singing is a physical reminder to the body that it has to attune itself to the present moment. In addition, the music was shared by these students regardless of their age. The assumption was that no matter how old you got, you were still capable of enjoying and participating in music, or oral language. By focusing on activities that were shared among all children, regardless of grade level, one-room schools not only created an acute sense of audience, but they reinforced a valuable lesson about the nature of learning: some things one never outgrows.

The architecture of one-room schools made it impossible to segregate students by grade level, at least in the strenuous mode that we use now. The lesson to be learned from their fluidity is that the human mind is not an empty box waiting to be filled by the requisite "stuff" of first, second, fifth, or tenth grade. Our brains are organisms that evolve, grow, atrophy, or quicken depending on what they encounter. One-room schools did not by

their nature guarantee a lively or impassioned encounter. But they did require students to engage in this encounter in the company of both older and younger students. That pressure was a powerful reinforcement to the authority of the instructor.

The single greatest feature of one-room schools that our modern classrooms have come to validate is their emphasis on peer tutoring and cooperative learning. These terms describe the methods and strategies teachers use to garner more active participation from students. Skills of the slow learner are sharpened by the teaching acumen of the quick thinker. More students come to recognize the collaborative nature of thinking, problem solving, and reflection. These methods were built into country schools by necessity. But the words used to describe it by alumni are hardly as fancy. To them, it was simply a matter of "helping" other kids. It was part and parcel of going to school.

Early on in my research, I met a teacher who remembered his one-room school in western Iowa with such detail he could still recite the names of his eight classmates. When he mentioned one of them, his face broke into a smile and he began to laugh, saying, "I taught him how to read. The teacher was busy with the other grades, so Eddie and I found ourselves working in pairs during the hour devoted to reading. I didn't know what I was doing, but I was three years older, and it must have been important enough for him to please me, because he worked like a fiend to get through the primer. It wasn't until years later, when I was studying for my teaching certificate, that I realized that was the first set of lessons I ever taught."

Nowadays, teachers consider it an exemplary practice for students to work with others to review and reinforce what they already know and younger students are struggling to understand. By necessity, one-room schools made tutors out of all its students. This not only sharpened their skills, but reinforced the idea that learning is shared, given away, or used for the benefit of other people. Part of this fluidity came from the lack of privacy inherent in such classrooms. As the teacher went through the sequence of lessons for each grade, students working at their desks were either eavesdropping on material they had already mastered (reviewing), or being enticed by material they were just barely able to understand (previewing).

By organizing lessons "within earshot" of various grade levels, this curriculum allowed students to see the overall pattern and context for learning. They were reminded—almost daily—

about what they were supposed to know. And they were given the opportunity to imagine what they would be learning in a few months, or even a year's time. Thus, the setting of the one-room school reinforced the concept that students learn not by compartmentalizing lessons and concepts, but rather by understanding the patterns of knowledge and skill that develop over time.

These skills were tested not simply by the teacher, but by the presence of other students in the room who needed help. Peer tutoring and cooperative learning are nothing new on the scene of sound educational practice. For anyone engaged in mastering an idea or an activity, the surest way of seeing just how much you know or understand is by asking yourself to teach it to another person. In the words of the poet Theodore Roethke, "we learn by going where we have to go." And surely, one of the most timeless ways of "going" somewhere is by "teaching."

There are other catch-words in modern classrooms that were part and parcel of one-room schools, such as "interdisciplinary learning" and "individualized instruction." In these primitive classrooms, entomology was a science, an art, and a practice, depending on the season. A good teacher could instruct students in geology, biology, and chemistry simply by opening the windows and letting the weather in. At most country schools, students looked forward with glee to their time at the "work table," where they were left to their own imaginations to find something to read or study.

One woman I interviewed—who eventually became a teacher of modern languages—recalled with great fondness how she and a friend were given a French dictionary and told to learn as many words as they could. Of course such instruction was hardly schematized—most of us would cringe if we heard of a present-day teacher using

such a haphazard method. Nonetheless, those French lessons shared between these two young children "took." They were just the right combination of freedom and structure needed to see the pleasure and order of language study. And they inspired one young child to do the most important thing: continue to learn and feel that what she learned was her responsibility and keepsake.

How could the teacher of this child know she would grow up to become a student of languages, and eventually a high school teacher? Perhaps she had a hunch that the young child sparkled with English, and thought it was a good bet to give her the dictionary of another language to see what she would make of it.

Indeed, teachers in one-room schools had to be subtle interpreters of human nature in order to know when students needed review, help, or simply time to practice on their own. What helped in that knowledge was the consistency of the pupils. If a teacher worked in a district for several years, her students grew up under her nose, and it's quite likely that a successful teacher would learn both intellectual and personal temperaments of the class. Without question, some teachers were better at this than others, then as now.

Whenever I start to proclaim the validity of one-room schools, I'm reminded of a friend who once silenced me pretty abruptly by saying: "Listen, I spent my first five years in a one-room school, and I was bored out of my mind." Her cynical memory is a useful refrain to any of us who forget that no two students learn precisely the same way. Classrooms are laboratories of learning and good teachers are always on the lookout for the book, exercise, experiment, or field trip that will catch the imagination of a student and not let go. But there's no doubt that the one-room schools fostered more of a self-reliance in learning among students. At the same time, this experience reminded everyone that whatever was worth knowing or doing was worth being shared.

That sharing took on a ritualized, highly formal dimension twice a year, in the "pageants" or "exhibitions" put on by the students for all members of the larger community. Teachers can recount with fear the sense that this was the most serious "test" for their abilities. A mediocre performance could result in canceling a contract for the next year. But the idea of students being responsible for demonstrating what they had learned to a wider audience is one of the most basic of all assessment strategies. It reinforced the connection between the school and its community.

Fayette County

Fayette County

These schools fostered this connection in other ways as well. One family each day in the winter was sometimes charged with bringing a hot lunch for all the children. Water was supplied by a nearby farm if the school didn't have a well. In many towns, the school was the site of the Friday night literary societies.

In this way, one-room country schools were part of the flourishing democracy within the state of Iowa. Some critics might say that such schools served only the "middle" children with any success—that the truly gifted and intelligent were never rightfully challenged, and those with special needs could never be accommodated. But living in the middle is where most of us spend our lives, no matter how individual or idiosyncratic we each turn out to be. By fostering a sense of shared learning, by asking that students be critical listeners as well as helpmates, one-room school teachers transformed the lives and minds of thousands of children. They gave to Iowa its heritage as a state committed to education in the truest sense of the word. They made Iowa a leader in learning.

Photographs from Fayette County schools, 1951-52, taken by County Superintendent of Schools. Fayette County Historical Society

Fayette County, 1890s.

Is The One-Room School Concept Relevant Today?

Kathy Moe
Lewis Central Community School District, Council Bluffs

It is vital that educators rethink the structure of schools because of the change in demographics of our society, and in the expectations for public schools. A promising model for breaking away from the rigid structure of single-grade classrooms where teachers do most of the talking, is the one-room schoolhouse. Teachers in one-room schools had to attend to the needs of students in seven or eight grades. They could not spend their time standing up front talking to all the children at once. These teachers helped students on an individual or small-group basis, and older students worked with younger ones. Students took action for their own learning because they could not always count on the teacher's help every minute of the day.

What was a matter of necessity in rural America years ago is a better way of organizing learning today, as the recent brain research reveals. Children learn in different ways, and at different rates, and they do this best by being actively involved in their learning.

Multiage classrooms can be like modern day one-room schoolhouses, with children of a variety of ages and abilities working in different groups and in different ways. Teachers in multiage classes can design instruction to the way children really learn, because of greater flexibility in how they group and teach their students.

As an early childhood teacher I can tell you that an age difference of eight months or a year is enormously important in a child's development. It makes no sense to group children according to their chronological age and then teach them as if they are a homogeneous group. This can be true for older students also. Some can learn much more than students their age are usually taught, while others can be several grades behind. Plus, some students are verbal/linguistic learners and do it best by reading and others need instruction that is more visual or hands-on.

The kind of teaching that worked in the one-room schoolhouse takes advantage of the normal differences among children. Multiage classrooms lend themselves to that kind of teaching. Students in multiage classes take responsibility for their own learning and that of their classmates because they can work alone and in large and small groups. Because the classroom is without long lectures and worksheets made for the whole class, children have more freedom to move at their own rate and in their own way. Teachers can then become facilitators and mentors instead of being the source of all the answers.

Multiage classrooms need to be part of broader school reform efforts because they involve fundamental changes in the way schools are run. Now is the time to do it because we have an advantage over the one-room schools of the past: technology, which will allow the teacher to design instruction to meet the needs of individuals and groups of children.

How many adults spend their days working with people who are exactly their age? Not very many I would say, so why should children? Multiage classrooms support the likes and differences between children that have nothing to do with age. Multiage classrooms can help ensure that all learn at their own rate and in their own way.

Fairview Independent School, Jackson County, 1956

Ludlow #2, Allamakee, 1953

A Country School Conflict

The biggest news story involving an Iowa country school occurred on November 19, 1965. That's when Oelwein Community School District administrators, the county attorney, the county sheriff, and a deputy attempted to pick Amish children up in a school bus to take them to school in town.

One of *The Des Moines Register's* best reporters—Gene Raffensperger—accurately reported that Amish children ran into a cornfield adjoining the school, but three hours later quietly boarded the bus and went to class in town schools.

Raffensperger's story was quickly forgotten, but Tom DeFeo's dramatic seven-column, page-one photograph of Amish children running into a cornfield was not. That photograph pricked the Iowa conscience. How could we treat children like this, people asked.

Iowa Governor Harold Hughes and legislators wanted to make sure the incident would never be

In 1967, a law that allows religious groups to seek an exemption from state school standards was approved. That law remains in effect today.

To help readers better understand this event, we are reprinting the November 20, 1965, *The Des Moines Register* front page that featured DeFeo's photograph, the article written by Raffensperger, and portions of page five from the *Register* showing children boarding a bus for the ride home after attending school in town.

We've also included an article by Erik Ericksen who, for many years, worked with groups requesting exemption from Iowa's school standards. Today, Amish children in the Hazelton area continue to attend school in the same building where this incident took place in 1965. A photograph of that school is included elsewhere in this book.

Amish School near Hazleton

Photo by Larry E. Neibergall

The Des Moines Register

The Newspaper Iowa Depends Upon

Des Moines, Iowa, Saturday Morning, November 20 ... Two Sections   Price 10 Cents

VIET BATTLE RAGES 6TH DAY

Amish Children Scamper Into Hiding in Cornfield

Amish school children scurry for hiding places in a cornfield near Amish School No. 1 to avoid being taken by bus to nearby Hazleton public school. It is one of two rural schools in the area operated by 15 Amish families. The fathers ... OTHER PICTURES: Page 3.

BELIEVE REDS ARE TESTING U.S. STRENGTH

Saigon Committing Regiment to Fight

After Tears, Anguish, Amish Attend Classes

By Gene Raffensperger
Register Staff Writer

HAZLETON, IA - Amish children fled frightened into a cornfield Friday morning when a school bus came to get them but three hours later quietly boarded the same bus and went to class in Iowa schools.

It was the first time in three years that these Amish children — your children — out of the cold had attended class under a ...

AEC INSPECTS 2 IOWA SITES

IOWA CITY, IA. — Iowa made its bid Friday for a $348 million atomic accelerator.

A four-man team ...

Feels Length Of Viet War Up to Hanoi

By Allan Boschar

$230,000 FINE FOR U. S. REDS

WASHINGTON, D.C. — AP ...

U. S. Set to 'Blow Whistle On Business and Labor'

By Edwin L. Dale, Jr.
New York Times News Service

'ALL AT STAKE,' RUSK DECLARES

Sew Hands On; Circulation Good

ARLINGTON, VA. — AP ...

Good Weekend To Be Outdoors

Potomac Fever
Reg. U. S. Pat. Off.

WASHINGTON, D.C. — Harry F. Byrd, Jr. ...

Attempt to Steal 2 Rare Stamps

LONDON, ENGLAND — AP ...

INSIDE THE REGISTER

End Secrecy On Job Lists

After Tears, Anguish, Amish Attend Classes
Gene Raffensperger
Des Moines Register Staff Writer

Des Moines Register November 20, 1965

Hazleton, IA.-Amish children fled frightened into a cornfield Friday morning when a school bus came to get them, but three hours later quietly boarded the same bus and went to class in town schools.

It was the first time in three years that these Amish children had attended class under a state-certified teacher, as do nearly all other Amish children.

The dramatic turnabout came here as a happy climax to a day of tears and fear for the Amish children.

The 28 Amish children sang German songs and "Happy Birthday" in English as they rode to school in the bus.

At school, they were met with warmth and friendliness by the other children who had arranged "hosts" and "hostesses" for each Amish child.

TRUANCY ACTION

This was the day that school and law officials decided to bring truancy action against the Amish and to bring the children in a bus to a school in Hazleton.

The day started badly. First officials could not find the Amish children at their homes.

Next, at one Amish private school, the children ran into a cornfield and remained hidden when school officials came.

Then, at the other Amish school, 14 Amish children who were being escorted to the bus broke in fear and scurried into a cornfield.

Finally, at 1 p.m., school officials went back to the Amish schools. This time the Amish children quietly boarded the bus.

BOYS PLAY BALL

At school they took part in classes and recess.

Some of the boys played basketball.

It was a clear, slightly crisp morning Friday, the day of showdown. It was a day in which emotional scenes piled one on another until those watching the drama thought they could stand no more.

County Attorney Harlan Lemon, who watched the children run, finally shook his head in sorrow and anger.

"We're leaving now," he told the Amish parents. "Please get your children in out of the cold. We promise there will be no more action today."

3-YEAR BATTLE

The Amish have been resisting state efforts for three years—efforts to force the Amish to comply with the state law on teacher accreditation. Some Amish send their children to schools taught by teachers with only eighth-grade educations.

Amish fathers have gone to jail and shrugged. They have been fined more than $10,000 and have said nothing. Friday the state moved to bring the children to school.

Oelwein Community School District's 54-passenger school bus No. 8 rolled south out of Oelwein at 7:30 a.m. Friday. Aboard were Superintendent Arthur Sensor; Mrs. Donna Story, a school nurse; and driver Robert Hankins.

The bus stopped in Hazleton and picked up a fourth passenger, Owen Snively, principal of the Hazleton school and on this day the district's truant officer.

THE FIRST STOP

The bus went south of Hazleton, west on a gravel road, then south on a dirt road to the home of Christ Raber, Amish father.

Snively and Sensor talked to Raber inside the closed front porch. Raber said his children were not at home. "They're not in the house?" was a question by Sensor heard outside the porch.

Raber's answer was not heard.

When Sensor emerged from house, he told newsmen, "There are no children here and he says he doesn't know where they are."

Observers recalled that the night before the Amish had been told the bus would be sent to their homes. Had they secretly spirited away their children?

The answer at William Schmucker's house, the next stop, was no. Schmucker said his children were at the Amish school.

"Can we pick them up there?" asked Sensor.

"That's up to you," said Schmucker. "I can't give you permission."

The bus stopped at the Amish School #1. It was locked. A knock on the door drew no response. Nothing.

"There aren't any children anyplace today,"

said Sensor as he climbed back on the bus.

Adin Yutzy's place was next. No children. "I think they're hiding," said Sensor.

Ben Borntrager was next. A dog barked as Sensor and Snively approached.

"She ain't here," said Borntrager when asked about a daughter.

Then Abe Yoder's place. "I understand it's your duty to find out where the children are," said Yoder, answering a question from Sensor. "If I didn't have a religious reason for this I would put the children on the bus," said Yoder. "We can't tell our children to go on your bus."

"Then we'll have to take them by force," said Snively.

"That's up to you," said Yoder.

Then William Borntrager—and no children at home. Then Perry Miller where a dog barked and a gasoline pump in a shed popped in the frosty cold of the morning.

"HAVE TO GO TO SCHOOL"

"I'm the truant officer and under the Code of Iowa I must tell you that your children have to go to school," said Snively.

"My kids are just not going on the school bus," said Miller.

"Are they in school?" asked Snively.

"I don't know if I have to answer that," said Miller.

Snively took a gentler tone as he said, "You know we could have just sneaked in at the school and picked the kids up, but we wanted to come to the house and tell you."

"I still say I'm not going to put my kids on the bus," said Miller.

"What would you say if we put them on?" asked Snively.

"Go ahead if you think you have the right to do it," said Miller.

Two more stops at Amish farms. Same results. Then the Amish school known as Charity Flats.

It was known that 13 Amish children were in this school Friday morning. But they were gone when the big yellow school bus arrived.

TALKS WITH OFFICIALS

They fled to the cornfields around the school. When Sensor arrived at the school he was met by Jake Schwartz, Amish farmer who owns the land where the school is.

Schwartz ordered newsmen off his land, then talked to Sensor and Snively. He told them that several youngsters under seven years old still were in the school. The state was not interested in these children because the state law does not cover them. The Amish knew this, too.

The others, 13 in all, who were of the age specified under the law, ran for the cornfields before the bus arrived. Sensor slipped into a field and talked with one boy.

Asked if he were going to catch those in the cornfield, Sensor said, "Frankly, I doubt if I can catch them."

One could look over to the cornfield and see black hats popping up and down in the brown background of corn stalks.

CLIMAX NEARS

Now the dramatic climax was approaching. The bus was heading back to Amish School No. 1, the place that had been locked and empty before.

This time four buggies and two horses were in the yard. The American flag was flying. The Amish were here this time.

Also there were some of their parents, including Yutzy and Yoder. They met Sensor and Snively at the porch, and shortly this group was joined by Lemon and Sheriff Fred Beier, both of whom had been summoned to the scene by radio.

The dialogue on the porch went this way.

Sensor: "Are you going to let us go in and get them?"

Yoder: "We will, we can't stop you."

Sensor: "Will they come willingly?"

Yoder: "That I don't know. I told my kids not to go willingly. I said for them not to struggle or get hurt, but not to go willingly."

Sensor, Lemon, Deputy Sheriff Tony Wengert, Sheriff Beier, Snively and nurse Donna Story entered the school. The door shut. The big yellow school bus pulled up in the road 25 feet from the schoolhouse door. The driver opened the door of the bus. It was empty.

It was 10:03 a.m. A horse snorted and stomped its feet in the yard. An Amish mother came out of the school. She was weeping.

Sheriff Beier came out of the school and asked newsmen to back off the school grounds to the road. The Amish were coming, and he didn't want the path crowded.

It was 10:19 a.m. and the door of the school opened.

14 COME OUT

They came out, the Amish children. The girls were wearing black bonnets and black shawls. The boys were in black hats and denim clothing.

They were all out now, 14 of them.

Nervous, not sure which way to turn or look, they milled in a tight little knot at the edge of the school yard. The big yellow bus was waiting. Its door was open.

Suddenly a voice, perhaps that of a woman, said: "Run."

The children scattered. Most ran for a cornfield about 35 yards west of the school. Some ran the other way and disappeared behind the school toward another field of corn.

Amish mothers on the porch broke into loud sobbing. No one moved for that instant. Then Deputy Wengert reacted. He stopped a boy. It was Emmanuel Borntrager, 15.

The boy wept. He talked to officers for a few moments, then Sensor gently led him to the bus. The boy faltered at the bus door. He wept and wiped his eyes with a handkerchief.

Sensor urged him to get on the bus and not to be afraid. The boy, a chunky lad, took a seat in the first row.

Lemon and Sheriff Beier went down the row in an attempt to encourage some of the children to come out of the cornfield. They were unsuccessful, although Lemon himself entered the field.

Wengert went another way and found Sarah Schmucker in a cornfield. At age 8 she was composed, but frightened.

At the sight of Wengert she broke into tears. The big deputy sheriff put his arms around the girl and comforted her. She buried her head on his shoulder and cried.

Later, Wengert brought her slowly back to the Amish school and turned her over, still sobbing, to the care of an Amish woman.

Yoder said the action of the children was a surprise to him. "We did not tell them to run," he said.

The search was finally called off with Lemon's announcement that the authorities were leaving and his plea that the Amish get their children in from the fields.

Amish youngsters board a school bus for the trip home after attending classes Friday afternoon at the public school in Hazleton. Boys who acted as "hosts" accompany the newcomers to the bus.

Religious Groups Continue One-Room School Tradition

Erik Ericksen
Iowa Department of Transportation

From the fall of 1961 until late November 1965, the country school in Iowa became the focus of a civil conflict with issues not unlike those that propelled America's great Civil War just a century earlier. In Iowa, the issues were also moral, social, and economic with strong religious overtones.

The state of Iowa had issued an edict that all children of compulsory attendance age must be taught by state certified teachers. The Board of Education of the Oelwein Community School District in Buchanan County imposed another condition that impacted the two country schools operated by members of the Old Order Amish settlement in Buchanan County. Specifically, they declared that the children attending those schools were to receive their instruction in a public school in Hazleton, a small community just south of Oelwein with which the Oelwein schools were consolidating.

The refusal of the Amish parents to comply, and the events that followed their action, were perceived and reported in a variety of ways with attribution given to several conflicting moral, social, economic and religious positions. This conflict came to a head on November 19, 1965, when public school officials tried to load Amish children on a bus and take them to the public school. This action highlighted what some Amish scholars believe was the root issue of the conflict—the desire of the Amish to have their children taught in 'neighborhood schools' by their teachers.

This event was, in political jargon, a classic "photo-op." Amish leaders, aware of the planned pick-up, had instructed their children to run upon the teacher's signal. The command came, in German which was the Amish primary language, as children were exiting the school to board the bus. Run they did, scampering into the cornfield adjacent to the schoolhouse. *Des Moines Register* photographer Tom DeFeo captured the scene for all the world to see. And it was seen, literally around the world, when the Associated Press transmitted DeFeo's photo to news outlets across the globe.

A subsequent attempt that day at transporting the children without their parents' knowledge was successful. Amish mothers, kneeling and weeping and praying, greeted the bus and officials the next school day. The problem was not resolved

and the continuing publicity continued to tarnish Iowa's image.

Governor Harold Hughes finally intervened and called for a moratorium. In the ensuing months, his office and the state legislature fashioned an amendment to the state's compulsory education law which went into effect on August 15, 1967. This amendment, often referred to as the "Amish Exemption," empowers the State Superintendent of Public Instruction to exempt members of a religious denomination professing principles or tenets differing substantially from those embodied in the educational standards law. The exemption would be initially for two years with the option for annual renewal conditioned, at the Superintendent's discretion, upon proof of achievement in specified academic areas. In addition to exemption from all the state's educational standards, the law also exempted the members from compliance with the state's compulsory education law, essentially lifting the requirement to provide any formal instruction by certified teachers.

Subsequent opinions by the Office of the Attorney General of Iowa have opened the door to religious denominations other than the Old Order Amish. Presently, the exempted groups operate 40 schools enrolling over 900 children. In addition to the Old Order Amish, who operate about 28 schools, groups exempted include Beechy Amish, New Order Amish, Mennonites, Dunkard Brethren, and Old Order River Brethren.

Several original public country schoolhouses have been, and continue to this day to be, school sites for some of the exempted religious groups. Included among those confirmed as original public schools are Friendship School and Middleburg School near Kalona. Operated by the Old Order Amish, both were put into public service in the early 1900s and served public school children until they became Amish schools in 1966 and 1972 respectively. In addition, the Cedar River School and the Deerfield School north of Charles City served public school children, and were for a time farm storage and community center facilities. Cedar River became an active school in 1994 serving children in a new settlement of Old Order Mennonites, Groffdale Conference. In 1996, expansion of this settlement created the need for a second school and the settlement acquired the Deerfield School and put it again into educational service.

Based on observations over time of all the facilities utilized by exempt religious groups for their educational purposes, it is believed that there may be another five buildings that were at one time public country schools. All of these are in Old Order Amish settlements: one near McIntire, one near Drakesville, and three around Milton.

Two public school districts in Iowa—Jesup and Wapsie Valley—also operate public school buildings for Amish students. Each of those districts operate three buildings believed to be former one-room country schools once used by public school students.

Evergreen School, Kalona

Amish School, Washington County

Amish School, Washington County   *Photo by Wilford Yoder*

25

Mennonite Country Schools

Deerfield School, Chickasaw County   *Photo by Jolene Rosauer*

Cedar River School, Floyd County   Photo by Jolene Rosauer

Deerfield School, Chickasaw County   *Photo by Jolene Rosauer*

Preserving Our History
And Memories

P. Buckley Moss
The Birthplace of the 4-H Emblem
Breckenridge School
Wright County

Preserving our Heritage

Tom Morain, Director
State Historical Society of Iowa

The job of historians, according to philosopher Herbert Marcuse, is to keep alive possibilities. Without access to the past, we are restricted to only those things that we can imagine out of our own experience. History opens vast new worlds to explore, where the people looked at the world in different ways and ordered their lives according to different priorities.

When my wife and I were graduate students at the University of Iowa, we attended a slide lecture on 19th century architecture in Iowa City. The professor took us on a tour of buildings that we walked past every day, and — WOW — it was if we were seeing them for the first time. Brick work designs, fancy windows, stone carvings. How had we missed them before? For the next couple of weeks, we were walking down the center of the streets trying to get a better view of the upper stories and corners. It was a wonder we weren't run over by startled motorists. It was as if we had been seeing things in two dimensions only until the lecture opened up the concept of depth and we realized that these buildings had a history, too. When their stories were told, these once-prosaic stores and offices became an exciting part of our morning commutes.

Historic preservation keeps alive one avenue of access to those to those "foreign" eras of past. Photographs, drawings, reproductions, and written descriptions have their place, but they are often poor substitutes for the real thing — the authentic artifact or historic building. A reproduction Civil War uniform may be a precise replica in every detail, but does not evoke the awe that one feels standing in the presence of an army jacket that was what a 19-year-old corporal was wearing when he waited all night for the Confederate charge at Gettysburg. One can read about the history of rural education in the Midwest, but there are voices that one can hear only by standing quietly in the middle of a one-room school when the windows are open on a spring morning. We need the real thing.

Within the past forty years we have also come to realize that we need to widen our scope. Once we saved only the most noble features — mansions, clothing and personal items of famous people, memorabilia from famous famous events. Recently, however, we have discovered our kinship with the commonplace, the stuff of ordinary life of ordinary people. We are a nation of more than the rich and famous. We are a blend of people from all over the world, and our history must include the stories of all of us. Everyone has a story to tell, and everyone has something to teach us.

Perhaps it is true that those who ignore history are condemned to repeat it. But it is probably also true that those who ignore the history are condemned to live without it, and in doing so, deprive themselves of a rich resource of new experiences. It is the challenge of each generation to preserve the historic legacy it has received so that our children and grandchildren will have the same opportunity to go exploring.

Bennett School, West Des Moines, Polk County

Restoration of Garner #3
Pottawattamie County

Original school, circa 1900

Moving, June 1997

Restoring the interior

Project Complete, November 1997   *Photo by Bob Nandell*

Penny Wright, Preservationist
Photo by Bob Nandell

Restoration of Williams School in Wayne County

The relocation and preservation of the 1869 Williams School, Clay Township, in Wayne County to the Round Barn Heritage Farm Association in Allerton.

Presbyterian Mariner Volunteers
work on restoration

Other Restoration Efforts

Pleasant Hill #6, Tama County, on the move

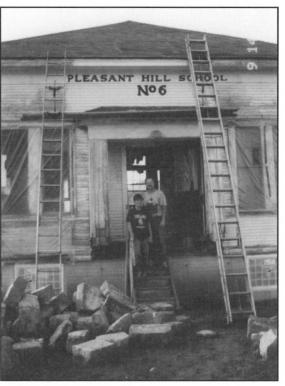

Pleasant Hill #6 at new site

Clutterville School, Hardin County

Friedrichsen School, Boone County

Portland #5, Kossuth County   *Photo by Bancroft Register*   *Bridgeport #6, Jackson County*

Cedar #7, Mitchell County

Fairview School, Franklin County

Sunnybrook School, Clay County

Converting a Country School into a Home
Plymouth County

Grant #8 in Plymouth County was a one-room school built in 1925 by a group of farmer carpenters. It replaced a smaller building that was not adequate to the Grant Township population. It was a square building, 28' by 28', that housed children in kindergarten through eighth grade. It was a pleasure to be educated in a country school because of the small classes where your learning was more individualized.

In 1975, we purchased the acre of property with the structure from my dad, who bought it in the late '50s or early '60s when the school closed. We added onto the existing building and now have a very comfortable and homey home of nearly 1,500 square feet, with everything we would want in a home, along with a two-and-one-half stall garage. We've never regretted doing what we did because the building was sound and built with excellent lumber and workmanship. We were fortunate enough to purchase an additional nine acres, so we now have some crop land, pasture, and a large garden.

We have a storm cellar (cave) in our house that goes from the basement, down a few steps, into our cave which is very convenient to store our home-canned fruits and vegetables. Since it's not very deep, potatoes don't keep well because it's not cool enough.

The coal bin in our basement is now a guest bedroom furnished with antique oak bedroom furniture.

Bill Osterbuhr, LeMars

Converting a Country School into a Home
Mahaska/Keokuk County

In 1941, we bought a small farm in Keokuk County with very bad buildings. Since farming was my husband's life, we figured we could pay for the farm and gradually rebuild all the buildings. We got the farm in fair shape and the necessary other buildings built with used lumber and our own ingenuity. The house was next, but the war had started and we couldn't buy material to build a house.

The opportunity came up that this one-room country schoolhouse was for sale. We investigated and put our bid in for it. We made the right bid and got the schoolhouse. We got busy, tore down the old house, and lived in the garage with our three children for several months.

We hired to have the schoolhouse moved and put in place over a basement which we had dug mostly by hand, then hired a man to wall up the basement. My husband, his stepfather, and I cemented the basement floor.

The schoolhouse made us a beautiful home. We divided the main room into two bedrooms with a closet built in between and a nice size living room. The windows are still the original windows in the bedrooms. The living room windows are also original except we divided the four and put a door between two windows on each side.

The entry door is original. It entered the cloakroom and room where coal buckets and the waterstand were kept. It is now our kitchen with replaced windows where the original windows were. The entry to the living room is the original entry to the main school room. We tore down the chimney and put it in the center of the house, as we heated then with a wood and coal stove. Later we put in a wood and coal furnace, then converted it to a gas furnace.

Since the interior of the schoolhouse had been painted with enamel paint, it was badly cracked, so we paneled most of the walls and lowered the ceilings. Later on, we added a utility room and bathroom, and also enclosed the original porch. The porch door is original, except we put glass in it.

We love our schoolhouse home. Several former students have stopped to see their schoolhouse turned into a home.

Mrs. Eva Landers, Delta

One Room Schools:
a Reminder of our Quest for Knowledge

Bob Nandell, photographer
The Des Moines Register

As if a lasting monument to Iowa's pioneers' quest for personal betterment and literacy, one room schoolhouses still dot our landscape.

Some are battered shells of what once was, some are used for storage of grain or agricultural chemicals, some are beautifully kept as museums, and some are still active parts of their communities serving as polling places, town halls, and 4-H meeting sites. Quite a few have even become residences because of their solid construction.

The fate of some of these stalwart buildings reads like the *Tale of Two Cities*. In serves as a polling place. One past presidential election saw it featured in *Time* with a handful of early-bird voters proudly standing by it.

Meanwhile, a similarly constructed schoolhouse east of Dougherty, Iowa, only a few miles south of the Scott Township building, is surrounded by growing brush and its unpainted siding sags a bit more with each winter's weather assaults. But still it stands, as a silent reminder of yesteryear.

But some of the things being done with restored one-room schoolhouses these days are fascinating.

As a *Des Moines Register* photographer I have witnessed the wide-eyed wonder of urban school children spending a day in the one-room schoolhouse at Living History Farms. The idea of a great black stove in the middle of the room for heat, and the idea that there are no computers, no media center and no specialized instruction leaves them in awe as they work with chalk and slates ciphering numbers and scribbling down verbs and nouns.

For these youngsters to realize that some of our nation's great industrialists, politicians, artisans, and teachers began their education in such humble surroundings at once makes them appreciate all the grand learning tools at their disposal today. Perhaps it makes them realize that if such greatness could be achieved with number-two lead pencils and shared rudimentary readers, their own potential is truly unlimited.

My own children participated in such a day, and came away talking excitedly about reciting the Pledge of Allegiance outside by the flag pole, and of using an abacus instead of a pocket calculator to figure out some math problems, and of metal lunch pails.

My wife still talks about playing as a child inside the one-room schoolhouse that once stood near the Floyd County farmstead where she grew up. Her father had attended school there until a multi-room brick schoolhouse was built in nearby Greene. There is something about these simple wooden-frame buildings that stirs a longing for simplicity in our educational structure, but yet gives us great appreciation of the gleaming new facilities that many youngsters enjoy now.

Furthermore, as voters ponder intricacies of school bond issues that may affect their property taxes by a few dollars a year today, these buildings remind us that simple turn-of-the-century farmers across Iowa provided real-dollar sacrifices in taxing themselves to put a one-room schoolhouse within walking distance of youngsters.

Perhaps it was the academic excellence achieved in one-room schoolhouses that proved to be their undoing.

As they produced the thinkers, engineers, and mathematicians of the early 1900s, the quilt-work of farms surrounding them changed dramatically. Farm populations thinned-out as agricultural machinery became more advanced, and as educations these schools provided enabled their graduates to fill positions in great urban industrial-age corporations, they became relics.

Now, in this age which worships things that are new, preservation of some one-room schoolhouses around our state may be far more than something nice to do.

It may be a social responsibility.

It may serve to remind us of how very basic educational experiences have ignited many a student's true quest for knowledge in our past.

Schoolhouse east of Dougherty in Floyd County   *Photo by Bob Nandell*

Scott Township Hall, Floyd County, 1993   *Photo by Bob Nandell*

Our Forgotten Heritage

Des Moines #2, Marshall County

Swamp Angel, Davis County

Winneshiek County

County Line School, Mahaska County

Wapello County

Copperhead School, Wapello County

Johnson County

Winneshiek County *Photo by John Deason*

Forest Grove #5, Scott County

Hancock County

Shell Rock #7, Butler County

High Lake School #10, Emmet County

Beckers Hardscrabble #2, Jackson County

Gillett Grove, Clay County

Cerro Gordo County

Carroll #8, Tama County

Clay County

Tingley #9, Ringgold County

40

Memories

Ruth M. Roach
Lucas County Morning Writers' Group

The one-room country schoolhouse
Stands abandoned and alone
With nothing left but memories
Of the past that it has known.

No laughter from the playground, now-
The iron bell is still.
Lonely windows reflect the sun
On that quiet country hill.

Not so much as a second glance
From the casual passer-by,
But those who remember the way it was-
Cast a wistful eye.

Alone it stands in the winter wind,
And under the summer sky;
For on the concrete highway below the hill-
A world has passed it by.

Iowans Who Attended One-Room Schools

Many Iowans who have made significant contributions got their educational start in a one-room school. Some are listed here.

• Norman Borlaug, Nobel Peace Prize Winner, Howard County
• Hamlin Garland, a Pulitzer Prize-winning writer, Mitchell County
• Tom Harkin, U.S. Senator, Warren County
• Bert Hickenlooper, U.S. Senator and Iowa governor, Taylor County
• Herbert Hoover, Iowa's only U.S. President, may have attended a one-room school in West Branch, Cedar County
• Nathan Kendall, Iowa governor, Lucas County
• Governor William Larabee taught in a one-room school in Allamakee County
• Weston Noble, Luther College choral director, Mitchell County
• Herbert Quick, writer, Hardin County
• Atlanta Constance Sampson, an artist who gained fame in New York in her 80s, Mitchell County
• Homer Seerley, President, Iowa State Teachers' College, Keokuk County
• Jessie Field Shambaugh, founder of the 4-H movement, Page County
• Dr. Dennis Spencer, chief of Neurosurgery, Yale University School of Medicine, Taylor County
• Laura Ingalls Wilder, author of the Little House on the Prairie series, Winneshiek County
• Grant Wood, America's best-known regional painter, Jones County

The Iowa Country School

Betty Cross, Lucas County Morning Writers' Group

It is impossible to describe all the country schools, as each had its own personality, but in general some of the characteristics were similar.

Most schools in the country were located near a crossroad on a one-acre plot. Many had a grove of trees under which the children could play games and eat lunch in good weather. There were very few items of playground equipment, as known today. Perhaps a teeter-totter or a rope swing, but mostly the games were of the tag, hide and seek, marbles, and Blind Man's Bluff sort.

Outside the schoolhouse, usually located near a back fence, were two small outhouses, or privies, one for boys and one for girls. This was long before the days of indoor plumbing. At many schools there was also a pony shed, where animals ridden to school were tied until time to go home. Some schools had a well and pump, where a bucket of water was pumped to take inside, but many did not have a well, and a couple of students would walk to a nearby home to bring back a bucket of water each day. This bucket, or the contents not spilled on the return, provided a common drinking source and usually a common dipper or tin cup was used by all. But this was not considered unsanitary, as the same methods were used at home, and many of the wells were located downhill from the barn lot.

Children walked to school, and many would cut across pastures and fields or down muddy or dusty roads depending on the weather. Some children would ride a pony, or might have a cart for several children, pulled by a horse or pony. A few neighborhoods would have a bus-like covered wagon and one of the neighboring farmers picked up all the children in that neighborhood.

Inside the school, hooks or nails on the entrance wall held coats and jackets and a bench or table made a place for lunch buckets. Lunch buckets were often a Karo Syrup bucket and held bread and butter slices for all the children in the family, perhaps some meat, and sometimes smashed cake or pie or a jar of applesauce. Fresh fruit was rare, and candy or cookies nearly unheard of. Poorer children had cornbread and often little else, washed down with a drink of water.

Some schools had maps on the wall that rolled up over the slate blackboard. The teacher's desk was in the front of the room and desks were lined in rows with children of each grade, or reader level, seated together. Some years there might be several to a grade, other years one or two students. Teachers gave assignments to each group and while one level read aloud or spelled their new words, another group worked on their assignment. If they finished, they listened in on the others. Spelling bees were contests that children eagerly studied for and the best students vied with the best from other schools.

Writing was practiced on slates, and a legible hand was highly desired. Arithmetic or numbers were done on the blackboard and erased, rather than using paper which was expensive. Very few extra books were in the library, and a good reader had usually read all the books available many times. Money raisers were held to get new books and they were eagerly awaited by each child.

Children learned by repetition the times tables, the counties of their state, the states and their capitals, the names of the presidents, and the continents and oceans of the world. Often there were rhymes or songs connected to these, like the alphabet song.

Schools opened with a pledge of allegiance to the flag, after the teacher had rung the brass bell which sat in the corner or on her desk. I am saying her, as though all teachers were women, but many were men, especially in the earlier times. Often the students were in their teens and nearly twenty and if the teachers were young ladies, just having finished Normal School, they were younger than some of the students. This sometimes led to discipline problems, and schools might prefer to hire a man who might teach in his off-times of another job. School terms were usually three months. Many students were absent, or the school was closed during planting and harvest, when they were needed to get the crops out of the fields.

A stove usually sat in the center of the room and those close might get quite warm, while those in the far corners were chilled. The teacher had to start the fire each morning and some student was assigned to bring in a bucket of coal or wood, and often to take out the ashes.

Hardly any schools had a piano, but a few had a phonograph to provide music. If the teacher was a singer, she might have a pitch-pipe and sing a song, then the children would learn it. These songs were sung at programs where each student had a part, and said a "part." It might be poetry, a small skit, or some other play. All the families for miles around attended these social events, and pies were sold, box lunches purchased, and speeches were given by the County Superintendent or other dignitaries.

Though the schools lacked many of the subjects of today, and had very little equipment with which to train students, many an important leader came from just such humble beginnings. Having less meant desiring learning more-more words to learn, more books to read, and a thirst for knowledge of places only heard of in a story. The country school, whether red or white, was the true anchor point of the rural neighborhood.

A Hit with the Superintendent
By Lois (Johnson) O'Reilly, Ida Grove

Country school teachers had visitors at times during the noon hour. The insurance salesmen seemed to use that time to try to sell insurance. One noon, while I was playing softball with the students, a man came. None of us knew him, but he said he would be the umpire so he stood behind the pitcher. When I got to bat, I hit the ball and it went straight out and hit him in the stomach. My first words were, "Kill the Umpire." When noon was over and we resumed classes, he followed us into the building where I found out that he was our new county superintendent. Needless to say I was embarrassed. After that, he and I had a good relationship.

Several years ago, I was pleased and surprised when I received a letter from a former student. She thanked me for being her teacher and for the lessons she learned, not only from the textbooks, but about life itself. She had read somewhere that you should take time out to thank someone who had crossed your path and made a difference in your life. After all those years, I really appreciated it. Out of those I taught, one became a minister, one a funeral director, one went into the electronic field, and some are farmers or housewives.

In all of them, I pray that I was able to instill something important in each life. I really feel as if I were blessed in many ways by being a student and then the teacher of the Good Old Country School.

From "Country School Memories," a book about Ida County country schools edited by Conley Wolterman.

The Day Dillinger Visited Us
Jean (Mathre) Biederman,
1st grade pupil at Mason #7,
Cerro Gordo County

On March 13, 1934, at about 2:45 p.m., it was recess time for the pupils of Mason #7 School southeast of Mason City. However, the teacher, Miss Pfunheller, would not let us go outside to play because there were three cars with several strange men on the road on the north side of our school. They appeared to be repairing something on one of their cars. We girls crowded into the very small girls' restroom and the boys into their restroom with a window in each room on the north. We tried to see what was going on. In a short time, the cars drove on.

After school, someone from the sheriff's department came by the school and told us that the men were Dillinger's gang who had robbed the First National Bank in Mason City. Betty Diercks, a second grader, was very concerned because she had recently deposited $5, a gift from her grandparents, and she was afraid it had been stolen.

My dad, Severt Mathre, came to pick up my sister Florence and me and he got a flat tire or two from the roofing nails which Dillinger's gang threw onto the road to avoid pursuit. Dad picked up a handful of the nails and our family still has these mementos.

After Dillinger robbed the bank and terrorized people in Mason City, he drove south 3 miles on Highway 65 with hostages on the running boards of the cars and they were instructed to look straight ahead. He turned east onto 130th Street and dropped off hostages one-by-one until the last one was released 1 1/2 miles east of No. 65.

After they repaired a car at our school, Dillinger's gang drove 2 miles farther east and then about 1/3 mile south to a sheltered area of a pasture on the Halvorson farm where others of the gang were waiting. They later departed through Hanford which was a mile south and a mile west of this hideout.

Student gift, Benton County, 1908.

43

Country School Outhouse

Bonnie Petty
Lucas County Morning Writers' Group

A country school outhouse was
A really popular place,
At least, in the good weather days.

It gave an excuse for getting
Out of class for awhile
Enjoying the breeze and the pretty blue jays.

But in the wintertime it was
A different thing for sure
For then no one wanted to go outside.

So we'd sit and suffer until
Our eyes were full of tears
To keep from freezing our bare backsides!

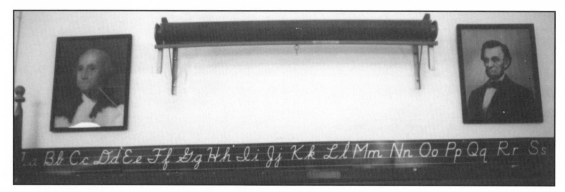

Washington and Lincoln

In our little schoolhouse
High upon the wall
Washington and Lincoln
Oversaw us all.

Did they hear our lessons?
Did they blame or bless
When we missed a question,
Made a second guess?

Time has passed and memory
serves the fleeting years,
Sometimes fraught with laughter,
Oft times touched with tears.

Still we see their vigil
As we oft recall
Washington and Lincoln
On our schoolroom wall.

Author Unknown

Country School

Frances Jacobsen Buckley,
former Sac County country school teacher

"It was the best of times...It was the worst of times."

There was something magical about the little old country school. When school convened in the fall, I remember the different fragrances of sweeping compound, chalk, and the freshness of the newly washed and starched white window curtains.

We had all grades from primary through the eighth grade. The teacher had to be a juggler or a magician to work all the classes into a daily or a weekly schedule.

The worst of times—we didn't have much in the way of material things to work with. Everyone tried to buy used textbooks for their children, and some didn't have books at all. Their parents deemed shoes more important than books, and they could not afford both. It seemed that there were always generous classmates who shared their books. Workbooks were unheard of at the time.

We sprinkled the sweeping compound on the floor to control the dust, and swept everyday. One spring morning I accidentally put up the flag upside down. I didn't know it at the time, but this is a distress signal. (We had no phone in the school.) Without realizing it, I had summoned three farmers from their field work. I guess that would qualify as my most embarrassing moment as a teacher.

Before a student could enter a high school they, as eighth graders, had to take and pass a state test over all subjects. The previous seven years were in preparation for this examination. No one slid by without knowing how to read, spell, figure, or learn geography facts. A student could fail just by having poor penmanship. This state examination motivated all eighth graders to do their best. If they failed to pass the tests, they were required to repeat the entire eighth grade. Plus it was shameful to them. Many a pupil said silent prayers while waiting for the results of the examinations. Oh, yes! Prayer was favorably looked on in the school. In fact, each school day began with a prayer and our pledge to the flag.

Former country school teachers at Reading School, Ireton, Sioux County   N'WEST IOWA REVIEW/SHELDON

1890 8th Grade Graduation Test

No new list will be printed until next February. Old lists will be sent you upon application, for additional examinations.

The annual reports in our hands, a larger number than usual at this date, indicate much painstaking care in their preparation. If those not yet here are sent soon and are complete and correct in the same degree, the laborious task of verifying all the work, securing corrections by correspondence, and afterwards compiling the tables for the printer, will be greatly lightened, and it may well be presumed that our summaries this year will have still more certain assurances of correctness, because founded upon original returns of more than usual accuracy.

Please send us the lists of school officers for 1890-91 as soon as returns can be secured from the secretaries.

The state board of examiners will hold an examination for state certificates and life diplomas, in Des Moines, commencing December 30. We suggest that you commend to your more advanced teachers of well-known merit and successful experience, that they procure the state certificate or diploma. Professional skill, and marked ability in management, deserve this additional recognition. To this we believe you will heartily agree, and we hope you will encourage your leading teachers to make application. Further information or circulars may be procured by application here.

In accordance with section 1577, all the county superintendents are hereby called to meet in convention at Des Moines, December 30 to January 2, inclusive. It is expected that every county superintendent will be present, unless attendance is absolutely impossible.

HENRY SABIN,
Superintendent of Public Instruction.

DES MOINES, IOWA, OCTOBER 21, 1890.

PRELIMINARY QUESTIONS.

(Every applicant is required to pay an examination fee of one dollar. See section 1769, S. L. 1888.)

(Any violation of the promises you make in answer to 7 will be sufficient to withhold your certificate.)

1. Give your name, age, post-office address, and state the number of terms taught.
2. What professional training in normal schools or institutes have you received?
3. What higher schools have you attended, and how long?
4. What professional books have you? Have you read them; and what others have you read?
5. What educational journal do you take?
6. What class of certificate, if any, do you now hold?
7. Will you promise neither to give nor to receive aid during this examination?

INCLOSE ONE DOLLAR WITH THIS PAPER.

PENMANSHIP.

1. Give the elements of the small letters; the capitals; name them.
2. Classify the small letters, slating the basis of classification.
3. Classify the capital letters, stating the basis of classification.
4. Name the space lines and describe the slant used in penmanship.
5. Describe the mode of teaching writing in a primary class.
6. Give a general outline of your method of conducting writing classes.
7. Name the requisites of a good business hand.
8-10. Write twenty lines illustrating the use of capitals, punctuation, and quotation marks.

GEOGRAPHY.

1. Name the river basins of North America.
2. Give the geographical position of France, its form of government, its climate and leading productions, three important cities, two rivers.
3. Mention three modifications of climate. Compare the eastern and western shores of this continent as to climate.
4. What are the dikes of Holland? Why were they built? Describe briefly the levees of the lower Mississippi.
5. Describe an all water route from Liverpool to Constantinople.
6. Name five agricultural and five mineral productions of the United States and tel where each is produced.
7. Name five countries bordering on the Argentine Republic.
8. What form of government has Russia? England? France? Mexico? Brazil?
9. How are tides produced? Give a remarkable example of tidal action.
10. What bodies of land does Behring strait separate? What bodies does it connect? How has it figured in national history?

ORTHOGRAPHY.

1. Define orthography, letter, and alphabet.
2. Name three valuable uses of the dictionary.
3. What are the leading uses of silent letters?
4. What is a substitute? Name three substitutes for long a.
5. Define word, root, derivative, prefix, and suffix.
6. Write three synonyms for each of the following: Merry, agile, timid.
7. What are the merits of written spelling exercises? How would you conduct such an exercise?
8-10. Twenty-five words dictated by examiner, and written by applicant.

READING

The true greatness of a nation cannot be in triumphs of the intellect alone. Literature and art may widen the sphere of its influence; they may adorn it; but they are in their nature accessaries. The true grandeur of humanity is in moral elevation, sustained, enlightened, and decorated by the intellect of man. The truest tokens of this grandeur in a State are the diffusion of the greatest happiness among the greatest number, and that passionless, God-like justice which controls the relations of the State to other States, and to all the people who are committed to its charge.

It is a beautiful picture in Grecian story that there was at least one spot, the small island of Delos, dedicated to the gods, and kept at all times sacred from war, where the citizens of hostile countries met and united in a common worship. So let us dedicate our broad country. The temple of honor shall be surrounded by the temple of concord, so that the former can be entered only through the portals of the latter; the horn of abundance shall overflow at its gates; the angel of religion shall be the guide over its steps of flashing adamant; while within, Justice, returned to the earth from her long exile in the skies, shall rear her serene and majestic front. And the future chiefs of the republic, destined to uphold the glories of a new era, unspotted by human blood, shall be "the first in peace, and the first in the hearts of the countrymen."—From The True Grandeur of Nations, by CHARLES SUMNER.

1-2. What can you say of the author of the above extract?

3-4. Explain clearly, as you would require from a class, the meaning of true grandeur of humanity, temple of concord, portals, adamant, chiefs of the republic.

5-6. What five questions would you ask in in order to bring out the meaning of the last sentence but one?

7-8. Same, of the last sentence?

9. Name five questions you would ask after the class have studied and read aloud the above section selection, to determine how well they understood what the speaker intended his listeners to think and feel.

10. What sentiment is this extract calculated to impress upon the mind?

THEORY AND PRACTICE

1. Give your plan for the organization of your school.

2.. What are the objects of punishment? What are proper punishments? What are improper punishments?

3. What is your method of awakening a spirit of investigation among your pupils?

4. What important literary qualifications should the teacher possess?

5. What do you understand by aptness to teach?

6. When and how do you prepare for conducting your recitations?

7. Describe the personal habits of a model teacher.

8. Should pupils be kept after school hours for any purpose whatever? Give reasons for your answer.

9. Name and describe the faculties of the mind in the order of their development.

10. What virtues should the children be taught to cultivate, and what vices to shun? How may the teacher do this?

ARITHMETIC

Note to the Examiner. Simply the answers to these questions should not be deemed sufficient. The object is not to test alone the knowledge of the candidate, but also his ability to explain and illustrate to his class.

1. Express decimally 3-800, 2-5 of 1 per cent, 85%.

2. Find the prime factors of 168, 264 and 696. From these prime factors find the greatest common divisor and the least common multiple of the given numbers.

3. What are two-ninths of 28 bushels, 3 pecks, 7 quarts, 1 pint?

4. Required the cost of laying a pavement 5⅓ rods long and 8 feet, 6 inches wide, and $1.40 per square yard.

5. If 3 be added to both terms of the fraction 5-6, will the value be increased or diminished, and how much? Explain as you would to a class.

6. Multiply 24.234 by .346 and write the result in words.

7. A school-house is built at an expense of $5,986, to be defrayed by a tax upon property valued at $665,870. What rate upon $1 of assessment will cover the cost?

8. Property worth $6,000 is insured for ¾ of its value, at ¾ of 1 per cent. What will be the loss, including premium, in case of total destruction by fire?

9. Make and solve a problem illustrating the application of percentage to the finding of an agent's commission.

10. What is due to-day on a note given September 24, 1887, for $138.50, interest at 5 per cent per annum?

PHYSIOLOGY.

1. Define anatomy, physiology, hygiene, a tonic, a stimulant.

2. In what ways is the bony structure of the body of great value? How are the bones nourished?

3. In what manner are large muscles attached to the bones? Describe briefly the microscopic structure of muscular tissue.

4. Name, in a natural order, several organs of circulation. What is the value of the very large number of minute capillaries in the lungs?

5. How is the wear and tear of the body provided for? How are the joints lubricated? What are the lymphatics?

6. What great dangers in the use of narcotics and stimulants? Why is the general use of opiates undesirable?

7. Speak of the connection between the climate and occupation of the individual and the choice of food. Name some of the beneficial results from the use of the fruits and grain foods, in Iowa.

8. Why is the use of tobacco, in any form, by the young, so very injurious? Answer specifically as to the organs and functions affected.

9. How do you ventilate a school-room? What indications will often lead you to observe the necessity for better ventilation?

10. Outline a brief lesson for a class in third reader, on the composition, characteristics, general uses, and common effects of alcohol.

U. S. HISTORY

1. In what way was the name of John Ericsson connected with an event of the civil war? What has revived his name and memory during the past year?

2. Comment upon the relative position of the United Stated to-day among the great powers of the world. Wealth, resources, army, nave, institutions, manufactures, intelligence of the people.

3. Name some of the important inventions that have been made by Americans.

4. Name four distinguished generals who afterward became Presidents of the United States. Cite some important measure connected with the administration of each.

5. Give two reasons for the rapid growth of California. Tell what you can about Gen. Fremont in this connection.

6. Name three prominent centennial celebrations, and give the date of each. What State is called the Centennial State? Why so called?

7. Who were the first explorers of the Mississippi Valley? Give some account of one of these adventures.

8. What two Iowa men, prominent in national history, have died very recently?

9. What people settled Acadia? What poem was founded on this bit of history, and by whom written?

10. Mention two prominent journalists, two historians, two prose writers, and two poets, whose names have been associated with U. S. history since 1800.

GRAMMAR.

They advanced in two lines, quickening their pace as they closed toward the enemy. A more fearful spectacle was never witnessed than by those who beheld these heroes rushing to the arms of death. At the distance of twelve hundred yards the whole line of the enemy belched forth from thirty iron mouths a flood of smoke and flame, through which hissed the deadly balls. Their flight was marked by instant gaps in our ranks, by dead men and horses, by steeds flying wounded and riderless across the plain.

1. Select three principal and two subordinate clauses.

2. Select two nouns each of which is the object of a verb, and three nouns each of which is the object of a preposition.

3. Select three adverbial phrases and two adjective phrases, state what each modifies.

4. Parse who. Give syntax of balls.

5. Conjugate the verb fly in the progressive form of the indictive mode, present tense. Decline which.

6. Give the modifiers of belched. Select a verb used in the passive voice.

7. Read the above extract carefully, to get all the ideas. Then recompose is, using your own words as far as possible.

8. The landscape which fills the traveler with rapture, is regarded with indifference by him who sees it every day from his window. Analyze.

9. What preliminary instruction should be given before technical grammar is taught?

10. Of what advantage is an accurate knowledge of the English language to the business man? Write an application for a position in a bank.

A Century of Change

The table below summarizes some of the key Iowa school statistics and state population totals. We've included the year 1901 because that was the year Iowa had the most one-room or ungraded schools in operation. We've also included the year 1896 and 1996 to illustrate some differences and similarities in Iowa education over this 100-year time span. The figures from 1896 and 1901 are from the 1901-1903 Biennial Report of the Superintendent of Public Instruction. The numbers for 1996 were obtained from the Iowa Department of Education.

Iowa Public School Statistics	1896	1901	1996
Number of ungraded, one-room schools	12,526	12,623	6
Number of school buildings	13,686	13,922	1,556
Average number of days taught	160	160	180
Value of school buildings	$15,867,425	$18,223,749	$5,334,929,290
Enrolled in school	543,052	562,662	502,343
Average daily attendance*	345,242	373,547	473,471
Average number of students per teacher	30	29	16.6
Male teachers employed	5,814	4,757	10,093
Female teachers employed	22,507	24,088	22,267
Total teachers employed	28,321	28,845	32,360
Average monthly salary males	$38.28	$41.53	-----
Average monthly salary females	$32.32	$30.68	-----
Average monthly salary all teachers			$3,697
Total spent on schools	$8,271,530	$9,321,652	$2,509,978,316
Total state population		2,231,853	2,851,792

*No compulsory attendance law prior to 1902

Wiegert Prairie Farmstead

Photo by Pocahontas County Conservation Board

Teaching about Iowa's Country Schools

Dee Altheide, Bloomfield, Davis County

Below is a summary of how a Davis County (Bloomfield) high school history teacher got students involved in learning about one-room schools in the county.

Note: The students that I worked with were high school age, alternative school students; they had dropped out of school, but returned. They had failed history and were in need of a credit in this area. Interest level was minimal, therefore the project evolved hoping to promote interest and provide learning experiences that would be of value to them now and in the future.

Objectives: Acquaint students with local one-room schools and where they were located and operated, within the county.

Activities: Name and locate one-room schools on a county map. The county provided a four-foot county map which was laminated upon completion of the project. (A picture of an old school was made and placed on each site location, using the lower right-hand corner of the picture for actual site location.) Students did the computer work of enlarging the picture used and making it in color.

Find when the schools began by searching in the land grant books in the local courthouse for the date when the land was given for the school. The staff in the auditor's office explained the way to locate what they were looking for and the students got so they were good at reading and locating the material. They also learned about recording and the difference between townships and sections. They soon became aware that some townships were better than others at recording information. The handwritten records were very interesting to them.

Seek names of teachers and years taught in these schools. Local school district officials were able to furnish records.

Find former students who attended these schools. An ad was placed in the local newspaper asking people who attended rural schools in the county to respond with years of attendance and their teachers, and any interesting items about life as a rural school student that they would like to share. Students decided what to put in the ad and placed the ad. Ad returns were put on the computer with any additional information that was given.

Other activities:
• Visited a one-room school that had been restored as a museum.
• Made a book with materials compiled, including each township and their schools, date of opening and closing, teachers, students, and a picture of the building.
• Organized an open house to display and report on the material gathered.
• Set up a mock one-room school.
• Wrote and sent out invitations to school board members, those who had provided information, parents, and school staff.
• Set up display of map and stories of schools that were contributed.
• Displayed pictures for viewing.
• Answered questions about what was done.
• Planned and served refreshments.
• Videotaped the event.

Results: People continue to contact me, asking for and giving information and pictures. I am still working on this project and hope when completed to have information preserved that will be of interest to many, as well as historically valuable.

A Teacher's Prayer
Beulah Cockrum, Mitchell County

Each time before I face my class
I hesitate a while
And ask the Father, "Help me Lord
To understand each child."

Help me to see in everyone
A precious soul most dear,
And may I lead that child through paths
Of wonder—not of fear.

Help me to teach with patience
And wisdom from above,
That they may learn truths from thy Word
And wonders of thy love.

Historical Photos

Land Office School, Sioux City, Woodbury County

Marcus Township, Cherokee County

Rock Township, Cherokee County, 1890s

Sunnyside School, Emmet County, 1941

Battle Center, Ida County, circa 1917-18

Rock Township, Cherokee County, 1890s

Northwest Iowa

Mt. Valley #1, Winnebago County, 1909

Dean School, Kossuth County, 1947

Katter School, Hancock County, Thanksgiving 1904

Sunnyside School, Emmet County, 1914-15

Historical Photos

Newtown School, Pottawattamie County, 1956-57

Scott Center School, Montgomery County, 1902

Ewalt #3, Carroll County

Sheridan #3, Carroll County

Guthrie Center, 1942

Monona County, 1941

52

Southwest Iowa

Templeton Independent, Carroll County

Mt. Hope School, Montgomery County, early 1900s

Maplehurst School, Montgomery County, early 1900s

Summit School, Nodaway Township, Page County, 1909

Allerton School, Wayne County

Historical Photos

Horse-drawn hack, Austinville, Butler County

Summit School, Eagle Township, Black Hawk County, 1885

Monmouth #5, Jackson County

Girls agriculture class, Geneseo School, Tama County, 1922

Northeast Iowa

Banner School, Chickasaw County, 1945

Warren #2, Bremer County,

Monroe #5, Benton County, 1902

Eastgate School, Jackson County, 1887

Historical Photos

Webster School hack, Keokuk County, 1928

Homestead, Amana Colonies, Iowa County

Oak Grove School, Van Buren County

Valley Chapel Pioneer #2, Cedar County, 1912

Cedar County, 1940

Wayne #4, Jones County

Southeast Iowa

Lockridge School, Jefferson County, early 1900s

Webster #9, Iowa County Scholars Reunion, 1870-1925

Zion School, Des Moines County, 1895

Bowman School, Johnson County, pre 1920

Pleasant Ridge School, Iowa County, 1910

Historical Photos

Madison County

Des Moines area, unknown location

Bear Creek Township, Poweshiek County, 1893

Iowa State Historical Society

Pleasant View School, Jasper County

Daily flag salute, Ackworth School, Warren County

58

Central Iowa

Jordan School, West Des Moines, Polk County

Hoosier School, Warren County

Palo Alto #8, Jasper County

The Little School, Palo Alto #11, Jasper County

59

Photos by Jack Grandgeorge

Jack Grandgeorge of Fort Dodge attended a one-room school in Webster County. From 1975-85 he photographed country schools in his travels in Iowa and southeastern Minnesota.

Boone County

Clay County

Hamilton County

Webster County

Webster County

Iowa's Country Schools
Today

© P. Buckley Moss

P. Buckley Moss
Grant Wood School
Jones County

Iowa is America's Country School Capital

This claim is based on the results of the county-by-county summary of country school stats developed for this book that documents the number of one- and two-room schools that are extant in the state and the number that have been restored and are being preserved as museums.

ISEA asked citizens in each Iowa county to identify the number of buildings remaining that had once been used as a one- or two-room country schools. We also asked the volunteers to describe how these schools were being used in 1997 or, if they were not in use, and were simply standing vacant. We also asked for a location and directions for getting to each of these buildings. We received complete and comprehensive information from many counties, and less detailed reports from others. The results are summarized in the table below.

These results show that there are more than 2,900 former one- or two-room schools standing in Iowa, and more than 180 of these buildings have been preserved as museums open for public viewing. Work is underway at more than a dozen locations that may result in the establishment of future museum schools.

Dr. Andrew Gulliford, Director of the Public History and Historic Preservation Program at Middle Tennessee State University at Murfreesboro is considered to be the most knowledgeable person on the subject of country school preservation. The third edition of his *America's Country Schools* book, published in 1996, includes a state-by-state listing of known remaining country schools based on research gathered from state historic preservation offices and interested citizens. This is the most recent attempt to complete this information on a national basis. Another research study conducted in 1997 by Mark W. Dewalt, associate professor of education at Winthrop University in South Carolina, revealed that several states have more operating one-room schools than Iowa. The states with the most are neighboring Nebraska with 120, and South Dakota with 66.

Based on the research just completed in Iowa, plus discussions with representatives from historic preservation offices in Minnesota, Nebraska, Montana, and Andrew Gulliford, we believe we can make the claim that no state can match Iowa's total of standing one-room schools and the number that have been preserved as museums.

County	Standing	Museums	Comm. Centers	Farm Bldgs	Homes	Vacant	Garage	Other
Adair	18	2	3		6	3		4
Adams	15	1	3	4	1	4	2	
Allamakee	37	3		12	9	8	5	
Appanoose	11	2		3	2	4		
Audubon	18	1		3	7	2		5
Benton	50		1	6	37	3	2	1
Black Hawk	29	2	2	2	16	1	1	5
Boone	18	1	3	3	1	6	1	3
Bremer	20	2				11	3	4
Buchanan	31	1		5	3	6		16
Buena Vista	17	3	1	9	4			
Butler	55	1		27	24	2		1
Calhoun	21	1	2	8	3	1	1	5
Carroll	5	1			2	2		
Cass	6	1			2	2		1
Cedar	50	2		21	23	2	1	1
Cerro Gordo	27	2	1	2	14	8		
Cherokee	38	2	2	18	6	3	3	4

63

County	Standing	Museums	Comm. Centers	Farm Bldgs	Homes	Vacant	Garage	Other
Chickasaw	41	3			25	4		9
Clarke	34	2	1	4	9	10	4	4
Clay	41	2	2	7	25			5
Clayton	89	3	8	15	32	6	4	21
Clinton	23	1		4	14	3	1	
Crawford	8	3			3	2		
Dallas	4	1		2		1		
Davis	30	1	3	4	14	7		1
Decatur	58	2	2	26	8	14	4	2
Delaware	7	2			2	3		
Des Moines	20	2		1	7	6		4
Dickinson	9	1		1	4	1		2
Dubuque	22	3		3	8	7		1
Emmet	9	1		4	2	2		
Fayette	76	3	3	6	31	8	8	17
Floyd	23	1	3	2	12			
Franklin	7	3	2			2		
Fremont	14	1		5	2	4		2
Greene	17	1	3	1	4	5	1	2
Grundy	62	2	1	14	37	5		3
Guthrie	21	2	7	6	2	4		
Hamilton	9	2	1	1	1	2		2
Hancock	19	1		2	5	7		3
Hardin	28	2		8	9	3	3	3
Harrison	24	2	1	6	9	3	3	
Henry	24	4	3	4	11	2		
Howard	51	3						1
Humboldt	33	1		5	24	2		1
Ida	9	1	1		3	1		3
Iowa	65	1	6	15	18	5		3
Jackson	35	3	3	15	10			4
Jasper	42	1		7	29	1		4
Jefferson	58	3		24	10	10	4	7
Johnson	14	2	2	2	6	2		
Jones	32	3	2	9	15	2		1
Keokuk	33	1		20	5	6		1
Kossuth	49	2		6	19	8	8	6
Lee	80	4						
Linn	54	3	1		35			3
Louisa	20	2	1	6	4	2	2	3
Lucas	30	2						1

County	Standing	Museums	Comm. Centers	Farm Bldgs	Homes	Vacant	Garage	Other
Lyon	23	1		4	6	5	3	4
Madison	9	3	2	1	1	1		
Mahaska	33	1	1	7	14	7		3
Marion	14	1		5	5	3		
Marshall	8	1			5	2		
Mills	6	1		1	2	1		1
Mitchell	48	2		15	22	6	1	2
Monona	16	1		5	5	4		1
Monroe	21	1	1	2		9		8
Montgomery	34	1	1	7	16	6	1	2
Muscatine	25	1	1	3	13	2		4
O'Brien	23	2		2	13	3	3	
Osceola	25	1		20	4			
Page	26	2		2	4	7		11
Palo Alto	15	1	3	1	7	1		2
Plymouth	28	3	1	5	12	3	2	2
Pocahontas	39	2		14	18		3	2
Polk	14	2			7			5
Pottawattamie	6	3	1					2
Poweshiek	6	1	3					
Ringgold	37	2		8	15	7		5
Sac	4	1			2	1		
Scott	44	4	3	4	26	3		4
Shelby	12		3	2	2	2		3
Sioux	63	4		14	34	7		4
Story	53	4		13	34	2		
Tama	25	0	1	8	8	4	2	2
Taylor	33	1	1	7	4	11		9
Union	23	3	1		11	6		2
Van Buren	11	5			2	2		2
Wapello	26	0		2	10	10	2	2
Warren	26	1	1	8	11	2		3
Washington	44	3			9	6		26
Wayne	14	2	1	2		6		3
Webster	25	1						
Winnebago	42	3	1	9	25		4	
Winneshiek	80	3						
Woodbury	47	7		13	22	1	3	1
Worth	81	1		21	43	8	4	4
Wright	12	3	1	2	2	5		
TOTAL	2,911	188	101	563	1,039	350	82	296

At least 18 former country schools are standing in Adair County. Three of the buildings—Eureka #5, Grove Center #5, and Prussia #5—are used as community centers and polling places.

Eureka #5 is located 8 miles south of Adair on N54 from Interstate 80.

Grove Center #5 is 3 miles north of Greenfield, then 2 miles east and 1 mile north on P21.

Directions for Prussia #5 are 3 miles west of Greenfield on Highway 92, then north 5 1/4 miles on N77 to the intersection of G35.

Harrison #8 (Prior School) is operated by the Adair County Historical Society. It is located off Highway 92 on the west edge of Greenfield.

Grand River #3 has been moved to the Adair County Fairgrounds and is maintained as a museum. It is open during fair week in late July. For 14 days in the fall, children from area schools attend class at the school where they are taught by former rural school teachers in an experimental local history project. The fairgrounds entrance is east of Greenfield and 1 mile north of highway.

Walnut #5 has been converted to a home, but the original bell tower is maintained. It's located west of Casey off Interstate 80, 2 miles south on N77 at the intersection of G15.

Compiled by
Beverly Speed
408 SE Linn Drive
Greenfield, Iowa 50849

Sommerset #5

Adair County Historical Society—Harrison #8

Jefferson Center, 1941

Grove Center #5

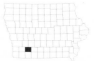

At least 15 one-room schools remain in Adams County. Three of the schools were moved from Washington Township to Mt. Etna in 1950. Washington #6 is used as a township meeting hall and polling place. The other schools are used for storage.

Grant #5 is also used as a township polling place. Quincy School is used as a township meeting place. It is located on the old Quincy Courthouse Square, established when Quincy was the county seat.

Four other schools are vacant, three are used as farm buildings, and another has been converted to a home.

Icarians built a "colony" school in the late 1860s. When the colony decided to split in 1878, a district court judge ruled the school had to be moved to a site halfway between the old and new colonies.

Today the colony school has been restored and is preserved as a museum building in Corning.

Compiled by
Saundra Leininger
710 Davis Avenue
Corning, Iowa 50841

Icarians School

Washington #2

Washington #6 (left), Washington #9 (middle)

If you would like to rent a country school museum, you can do it in Allamakee County.

Liston #4 retains its original decor. It is maintained by George Ashbacher in honor of his mother who taught the last four years the school was open. The school has original furnishings and a record of previous students. Rental information can be obtained by contacting Ashbacher at 416 Highway 76, Harpers Ferry, Iowa, 52146, or phone 319-586-2721.

Hanson School located on the south edge of Waukon is also maintained as a museum by Ray Sweeney. The school is open for display during Waukon's Threshing Days. The school stands next to the Sweeney House of Clocks Museum display. Contact the Village Farm & Home Store in Waukon to make arrangements to visit both the school and clock display.

The Little Red Schoolhouse Museum is located at the Allamakee County Fairgrounds in Waukon. The school was built in 1874. Nine years later it was painted red and has remained that color ever since. Over 100 teachers taught at that school during the 93 years classes were held there. The school is open during the fair and for students in the spring. It can be seen at other times by contacting the Allamakee County Historical Society members at 319-568-3439 or 319-568-2864.

Two schools—Hanover #2 and Lansing #6—are used as guest homes by the present owners. Another school, Lycurgus, is used as a rental dwelling. It is a two-story, stone rock structure located 6 miles north of Waukon on Highway 9.

Center #2 is currently used as an airplane hangar. Formerly it has been used as a township polling place and a snowmobile club house. The school, woodshed, chalkboards, and one outhouse remain. One side of the building was replaced by two large doors.

The Elk School is now used only for storage, but graduates of the school continue to hold reunions in September.

One of Iowa's famous country school teachers, William Larabee, taught at the Hardin School. Larabee went on to serve as Governor of Iowa from 1886-1890.

Compiled by members of the Allamakee County Sesquicentennial Commission and coordinated by Jane Regan 19 Allamakee Street Waukon, Iowa 52172

Linton #5, also known as Suttle Creek School, was moved to the Palmer Halverson Farm in 1956 and converted to a chicken coop. It took seven tractors and a D4 Caterpillar to pull and push it to its new location. In 1938, it was included in Ripley's *Believe It or Not* when all 16 pupils were Levenhagen children from three families.

The statistical breakdown for school usage is: two home workshops, three museums, three guest houses, 12 farm buildings, nine are part of homes, and eight are vacant.

Hanson School

Little Red School

Hanover #2

The Lycurgus School is one of the few two-story stone schools left in Iowa.

Photo by Denny Rehder

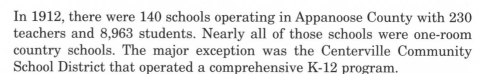

In 1912, there were 140 schools operating in Appanoose County with 230 teachers and 8,963 students. Nearly all of those schools were one-room country schools. The major exception was the Centerville Community School District that operated a comprehensive K-12 program.

The one-room school was a way of life in rural Appanoose County, depicting the energy and hope that charged through the rural towns and along the country roads, according to Daphne Keller, author of an Appanoose County history book.

In the spring of 1997, there were at least 11 one-room buildings remaining in Appanoose County. Efforts are being made to restore and maintain two schools—Fairview near Unionville and Erwin School near Cincinnati—as museums. Four other schools are vacant, three are being used as farm buildings, and two have been converted to homes.

Locations for some of the schools include:
Fairview School—there is a group now attempting to restore and preserve it; has been used more recently than most schools and is in quite good condition. Go west and northwest from Unionville on the paved road J13 for about 3 miles, then take gravel road going east and northeast for about 3 1/2 miles, turning left at both of the forks along the way; the school will be found on a hill high above the road by taking a left turn onto a dirt lane just before reaching the intersection.

Brazil School—now vacant but in fairly good condition and possibly used for some purpose. Go west from Centerville on Highway 2 for 3 miles, go north on the paved road T14 about 1 mile, take the first gravel road to the left and go 1 mile to the unincorporated town of Brazil; the school is in town on the south side of the road.

Sharon School—fairly recently used as a meeting place for Isaac Walton, now believed vacant; it is painted red and an outhouse still exists; go east from Centerville on Highway 2 for 2 3/4 miles; the school is on the northeast corner of the intersection.

Erwin School—now vacant with an attempt being made to preserve it. From the west edge of Cincinnati, southwest on Highway 5 for about 1 1/2 miles, then take a gravel road to the east for about 1/4 mile; the school is set back about 500 feet on the south side of the road.

Boston School—now used as a farmer's storage building; from Exline, go south on paved road I-30 for 1/2 mile, then go east on a gravel road for 1 1/2 miles; the building is on the south side of the road.

Hilltown School—formerly used as a school in conjunction with the Hilltown Christian Church in the community of Hilltown. The church has discontinued operation; the school is now on the premises of a farmer and has been converted into a workshop. From Moulton, go south on Highway 202 for 2 1/2 miles, then take a gravel road west for 2 miles, then south for 4 miles, and then east by northeast for 1/2 mile. The school is on a hill on the southeast corner of the intersection, but access is only available by going over private property through the farmer's drive and an access trail.

Compiled by
Lois Harris
RR#2
Moulton, Iowa 52572

Fairview School

Taylor School (formerly in Davis County) now in Moulton

One school, Douglas #3, is used as a museum; and two former country schools, Leroy #3 and Leroy #8, have been moved to the elementary school yard in Audubon where they have been merged together and pressed into service as a preschool room.

Seven other schools have been converted to homes, three are used as farm buildings, two are vacant, one is used by the Brayton Baptist Church, one is used for storage in the former town of Oakfield, and another is used as a cabin beside a farm pond.

The "Little Red Schoolhouse" museum, operated by the Audubon County Historical Society, is located one mile south of Audubon in Nathaniel Hamlin Park. The school was built between 1865 and 1874 in Douglas Township.

Sometime before 1910, this building was moved by a team of eight mules to a farm 1 1/2 miles away. It was then used as a tool shed and granary. Charles and Joni Hansen donated the building to the historical society and it was moved to Hamlin Park in 1984. The historical society has restored the building and has added desks and books originally used in country schools.

Compiled by
Barba Jean Duvall
505 Brayton Street
Audubon, Iowa 50025

The park is open on Saturday and Sunday afternoons during the summer, and at a festival the first Sunday in October. Also included at this park site are a former county poor farm building maintained as a museum, windmills, old farm machinery, and wildflowers.

Hamlin #2

Leroy #3 and #8

Little Red Schoolhouse

Some 50 former one-room country schools are still standing in Benton County. Most of those structures—37—have been converted to private residences.

In 1946 when schools were consolidated, seven country school buildings were moved to Vinton and located on a football field near West Elementary School and used to educate the influx of students from the country. As student enrollment declined and there was less need for classrooms, those schools were returned to the country.

Today, in addition to the private residences, six schools have been converted to farm buildings, two are used as garages, one is being used as a woodworking shop, and three are vacant. Monroe #5, located 3 miles east of Dysart on 59th Street on a gravel road, is a community center that is used by the 4-H.

Another school, Benton #7 or Upper Stone, is listed on the National Register of Historic Places. Now used as a home, it is located 5 1/2 miles north of Shellsburg on W26 and 1 mile west on 58th Street Drive.

Florence #1, or Conley School, features a gable roof and unusual vestibule. It is used as a hog house and located 2 miles north of Norway on Highway 201, then east on 75th Street and east of 32nd Avenue Drive.

Compiled by several members of Railway, Agriculture, Industrial, Lineage Society (RAILS) of Vinton, including Mrs. Marge McDowell P.O. Box 186 Vinton, Iowa, 52349, and Mr. Al Schwartz

Benton #7—Upper Stone

Florence #1—Conley School

St. Clair #7

Two country schools have been restored as museums and work is underway to restore another school in Black Hawk County.

The Little Red School located in downtown Cedar Falls on First Street is one of the most active country school teaching centers in Iowa. Three one-week sessions are held for students during the summer. Students are exposed to the actual curriculum taught in country schools at the turn of the century. The school is open to visitors on Wednesday, Saturday, and Sunday afternoons 2-4:40 p.m. from May through October. Special events are held prior to Christmas.

Another building moved from Pocahontas County—the Marshall School—is operated as part of the museum facilities of the University of Northern Iowa. The school is used for some university classes and community groups can schedule meetings at the school. Special programs are conducted for students from area schools. For more information about the Marshall School program call 319-273-2188.

In Bennington Township, located north and east of Waterloo, 4-H members have adopted restoration of Bennington #4 as their community service project. Many township residents are working with the 4-H members to restore the school so that it can be used for township meetings and as a museum school for area students.

All told, a team of researchers identified at least 29 country schools in Black Hawk County. Some 16 schools have been converted to homes. One is being used as a gun shop and another has been developed into the D and D School House Crafts shop by a former Cedar Falls teacher, Donna Hoffman. The shop is located north of Cedar Falls from the NEITA racetrack, go 1 mile west and 1/2 mile south.

Compiled by
Ruth Rohm
2305 Valley High Drive
Cedar Falls, Iowa 50613

Center School in Fox Township and Washington #2 are used as township meeting places. Two schools have been converted to farm offices, one building is vacant, and one is being used as a garage.

Little Red School, Cedar Falls

Bennington #4

Marshall School

D&D School House Crafts

As an outgrowth of Iowa's sesquicentennial observance, the Boone County Historical Society put up signs that gave dates of operation in front of the former schools still standing in Boone County. This included 18 one-room country school buildings and five consolidated school buildings.

One of the one-room schools—Hickory Grove—has been restored as a museum and is furnished as a 1920s school or earlier. It is located in the Don Williams Country Conservation Park on county road P70, 6 miles north of Ogden. Several school groups visit this school and listen to presentations by former country school teachers. The school is also open on Sunday afternoons, June through September, from 1:30 - 4:30 p.m.

Another country school—Harmony—was once used as studios for Boone radio station KWBG. The radio antenna tower stands beside the school, which is located south of Boone on Story and Peach Avenues.

At least three other schools are used as community centers. They include:
• Berkley School—located in the town of Berkley
• Mackey School—in Harrison Township, located on 130th Street and W Avenue (also used as a polling place for elections)
• Fraser School—in Fraser, is used as a town hall

Work is continuing on restoration of the Friedrichsen (Vernon) School. In recent years the Lawrence Bice family has repaired the foundation, replaced the roof, and planted a grove of trees around the school. They hope to have the school open as a museum for school children to visit in the future. The school is located 9 miles south of Ogden on Highway 169 and 310th Street.

Six other schools are vacant. One, owned by St. Paul's Lutheran Church, is used for church functions and bible school in the summer. One has been converted to a home. Other uses for the former country schools include three farm buildings and one garage. Five consolidated buildings are located in Boxholm.

Compiled by
Mrs. Alvin Harten
1656 Deer Avenue
Ogden, Iowa 50212

Bryant School (Museum) in Boone

Hickory Grove   *Photo: Boone Today*

Harmony School   *Photo: Boone Times-Republican*

At least 20 former one-room schools in Bremer County were located following research in August and September of 1997.

Two schools are being preserved as museums. Warren #2 has been relocated to a city park on Main Street in Tripoli. The school is maintained by the city. It is open by appointment from May through October by contacting the curator of the school, Helen Brase, 319-882-4801.

The other museum school was built in 1881 by St. John's Lutheran Church. It was used as a school and church until the church was constructed. The school was restored in the early 1970s and was rededicated in 1976. It is maintained as a museum school and is used as a repository for church history. The school is open by appointment by calling 319-984-5767. It is located in the village of Maxfield by St. John's Lutheran Church north and east of Denver.

Two other schools are maintained by local residents and are used for reunions and social gatherings. They are Warren #5 and Douglas #7.

Another one-room school was built in 1871 by members of St. Paul's Lutheran Church. The building was originally used as both a school and a church. The school continued until 1963. Today that building continues to be used for Sunday school classes. The church is located in the village of Artesian near Waverly.

Eleven former schools have been converted to homes, three are being used as garages, and one is being used as a horse barn.

Compiled by
Peg Heidt
1120 2nd Avenue SW
Waverly, Iowa 50677

Franklin #2

Douglas #7

Warren #9

St. John's Lutheran School

Fifth-grade teacher Richard Krone spearheaded an effort that resulted in the establishment of a country school museum next to the school he teaches at in Rowley which is part of Independence School District.

Krone's father had restored a country school. Those memories rekindled his interest.

"We started talking with other teachers about the idea of locating a country school on our school grounds to use in conjunction with our program, and a teacher volunteered that her family had a country school on their farm," Krone said.

A successful fund-raising effort was undertaken to move and restore the Summit School. In September of 1996, a dedication ceremony was held for the school. Participants included Governor Terry Branstad.

The school has now become a popular meeting place for a wide range of age groups. And it has helped Rowley students better understand the role country schools played in Iowa's early history. "You need something tangible to help students understand history," Krone noted.

Hazleton Township, which is in the heart of the Amish country, is the township with the most one-room country schools in the state—14. One school is used as a town museum. It is located in the 100 block of the downtown area of Hazleton on Highway 150. The Amish operate nine schools and the Wapsie Valley School District operates three other one-room schools for Amish children. Another school is used as a craft shop by the Amish.

In Independence there is a little red schoolhouse that has been turned into a gift shop. It is now located on First Street West. Sumner School #2 is now being used as a playhouse for grandchildren on the Morris Greenley farm.

Six other schools are vacant, five are being used as farm buildings, and three have been converted into homes.

Compiled by
Richard Krone
216 First Avenue
Rowley, Iowa 52329
and
Gary Buresh
1875 Otterville Boulevard
Independence, Iowa 50644

Sumner School #2

Westburg #7

Little Red Schoolhouse

Some 17 former one-room country schools are standing in Buena Vista County. "There are quite a few country school buildings, long since blended into farmsteads and town homes, that we have not identified or located," admits Arne Waldstein who developed the school listing.

At one time more than 100 country schools were operating in the county. After serving rural students for over 70 years, the last country school was closed in 1949.

Three of the remaining known schools are used as museums.

A building from Elk Township is located in the Storm Lake city park. It is being restored as a turn of the century school. Another school is part of the railroad depot museum near Albert City.

Another school is maintained as a museum on the Thresherman's farm near Albert City.

Compiled by
Arne Waldstein
1522 West 5th St., Apt. 5
Storm Lake, Iowa 50588

Another school is used as the community center for Scott Township.

Four other schools are now used as homes, and eight others are used as farm buildings.

Elk Township located in Storm Lake Park

Elk Township School

Elk Township relocated—Storm Lake

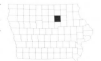

There are 55 former country schools remaining in Butler County and at least six other schools have been moved from the county to other locations and are still in use. At one time, 141 country schools were operating in the county.

Some 24 schools have been converted to homes, 27 are used for farm buildings, and two are vacant. Another school is being used as a Jehovah Witness Hall in Shell Rock.

Butler can boast of having the only country school painted yellow in Iowa that is operated as a museum. The school, Pittsford #3, was built in 1888 and painted white until 1916 when the color was changed to yellow. In 1957, the school was moved to the courthouse grounds in Allison, and for the next 39 years it also served as the Butler County Historical Museum.

In the spring of 1996, non-school related contents of the museum were moved to a building on the Butler County Fairgrounds. The little Yellow School continues to be used in the spring for a day of country school by area students. The school is open on a request by contacting Judi Poppen in Allison at 319-267-2255.

Compiled by
Ruth Hahn
210 5th Street
Parkersburg, Iowa 50665

Jackson Township #4

Ripley #4 in Aplington

Yellow School in session

Pittsford #3

Some 21 former country schools have been identified in Calhoun County.

The first school in Calhoun County was located near Lake City in 1856. The teacher was David Reed. By 1890, there were 141 country schools in operation. By 1959, all the country schools had consolidated with town schools and ceased operation.

Five of the schools have been converted to cottages located near North Twin Lake. Three sit side-by-side and are painted red, yellow, and green.

Four of the schoolhouses were moved into Knierim. Three are used as homes, and the fourth is now a garage at the New Coop Elevator in Knierim.

The Lincoln #1, Red Schoolhouse, built in 1916 and operated as a school until 1954, is now operated as a museum on the Manson Fairground Park north of Manson.

Center #8, known as the Ogle School, is used as a township hall and is located 3 miles east of Rockwell City on Highway 20.

Garfield #5 is used as a polling place for the township. It is located at the intersection of 250th Street and Fletcher, east of Lytton.

Sherman #5, located near an old cemetery and about two acres of native prairie grass, is 4 miles west of Manson on Highway 7.

Other former schools are being utilized as homes, farm buildings, garages, and one is vacant.

Compiled by
Katherine Treman
2137 NE Twin Lake Road
Rockwell City, Iowa 50579

Schools converted to cottages at North Twin Lake.

Lake Creek #6, closed 1957

Compiled by
Mrs. Marie Hackett
704 W. 15th Street
Carroll, Iowa 51401

At least five former country schools are still standing in Carroll County. Two have been converted to homes, two are vacant, and Maple River #5 has been restored and is used as a museum. It is located in Graham Park, 1/2 mile north of Highway 30 off Grant Road.

The school started operation in 1873 and was closed in 1947. Because this building was adjacent to a national highway (#30) and near a railroad track, hobos very often slept in the school. Former teachers say they were not frightened by these intruders, they expected them. The hobos kept the stove going all night which made it difficult for teachers to always have an adequate supply of coal on hand.

In November of 1966, the Kiwanis Club of Carroll moved the building to Graham Park. The Carroll County Historical Society now maintains the building. It is open for tours by appointment.

Maple River #5

Summerset #3   *Photo by Bob Nandell*

Bob Anderson likes to collect information about country schools in Cass County. He regularly writes a country school column for the *Atlantic News-Telegraph.*

Last winter, he asked readers to come up with the formal and informal names of all the former country schools that once stood in Cass County. He came up with a list of names for 117 schools. They included Crow, Hell's Half Acre, Maple Dale, Lone Tree, Sunnyside, Turkey Grove, Stony Point, Gold Hill, Toad Leap, White Cloud, Violet Hill, Studley, Stern, Swede, Was, Mayflower, and Victoria Center.

In 1960 the Atlantic Lions Club moved the Lone Tree School to the Sunnyside Park at the west side of Atlantic where it is used as a museum. It is open to the public on Sunday afternoons from 1-3 p.m., June through Labor Day.

Two other schools are used as homes, two are vacant, and one has been converted to an insurance office.

Hell's Half Acre has been converted to a residence. It is located 1/2 mile south and 1 mile east of Interstate 80, exit 57.

Compiled by
Robert E. Anderson
1606 Waddell
Atlantic, Iowa 50022

Bear Grove #5—Lone Tree School

Benton #5—Center School

Pymosa #2—Hell's Half Acre

Grant #9—West Railroad School

95

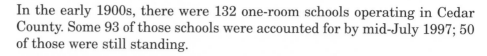

In the early 1900s, there were 132 one-room schools operating in Cedar County. Some 93 of those schools were accounted for by mid-July 1997; 50 of those were still standing.

Some 23 schools had been converted to homes and 21 were being used as farm buildings. Two are vacant and another was converted to a garage.

Reunions are held at Valley Chapel by graduates of that school.

The Red Oak #1, also known as Bedbug School, has been restored as a museum. The school was moved to the Cedar County Fairgrounds in Tipton in 1989. Volunteers worked on restoring the school for six years. It was open for public viewing in 1995. Mini-school sessions were held with former rural teachers conducting classes at fall festivals in 1995 and 1996. Various items including more than 150 books have been donated to equip the school. Country school is conducted for area students at this site.

Another school in the county maintained as a museum is the first West Branch school that Herbert Hoover may have attended. The school is located on the grounds of the Herbert Hoover National Historic Site near the Hoover Presidential Library-Museum. The school has been restored with furnishings to reflect the time period of the 1870s when Hoover was a student. The school is maintained by the National Parks Service and is one of four historic buildings and the Visitor Center on the grounds that are open to the public. There is a charge for individuals wishing to tour this site. Fees are waived for school groups. The Presidential Library and grounds are open from 9 a.m.-5 p.m. daily, except Thanksgiving, Christmas, and New Years Day. For information call 319-643-2541.

When the Bennett elementary and high school building was destroyed by a fire in 1943, seven one-room schools were moved into town from the country. They were pressed into duty as temporary learning centers until a new school could be constructed. All seven of the temporary schools are still standing. Five of them remain together converted to homes. Another school was moved back to the country and converted to a home. The final temporary school was moved downtown where it became an office for an electrical business. These schools were sold in 1949 for amounts ranging from $710-$870.

Compiled by
Delores Rohlf
P.O. Box 267
Tipton, Iowa 52772

Old Schoolhouse Block, Bennett

Red Oak #1

Hoover School, West Branch

97

At least 27 country schools have been located in Cerro Gordo County. In 1923, there were 105 country schools in the county.

Most of the schools still standing today, 14, have been converted to homes. One school—Grant Center #5—is used as a polling place. It is located west of Clear Lake on Highway 18 then north on S18 to B20 or 310th Street, then west to Dogwood Avenue.

A school moved to the Kinney Pioneer Museum complex on Highway 18 at the entrance to the Mason City airport is used for school classes in the spring. The five building complex is open to the public starting the first Sunday in May through September.

Another school, Owens Grove #3, is also used as a museum. Classes are held as they would have been years ago one day during the county fair. The school is located on the North Iowa Fairgrounds on Highway 18 west of Mason City. Eight other schools are now vacant. Two others are used as farm storage buildings.

Compiled by
Fran Tagesen, Director
Kinney Pioneer Museum
P.O. Box 421
Mason City, Iowa 50401

Teacher Salaries

"A teacher would rather teach in a town or consolidated school where they have only one or two grades in the room, and have the help and companionship of other teachers. On this account graded schools find it easy to take the better teachers away from the one-room school.

The rural school needs the better teacher at least as much as the consolidated and city school and can have her by paying an attractive salary. Schools at a distance from town will have to pay a better salary than schools close in to obtain a better teacher. The town and consolidated shcools of Iowa are paying $100 and up for grade teachers next year.

The most serious waste in the educational program results from the constant shifting of the teaching force. Of 105 rural teachers in Cerro Gordo County this year, 66 were teaching their first term in that particular district."

(Excerpts from the 1923 Cerro Gordo County Annual Report by R.E. Newcomb , county superintendent)

Grant Center #5

Portland #8—Hackberry School

Owen's Grove #3, 1930s

At least 38 former one-room country school buildings remain in existence in Cherokee County. In 1915, there were 131 country schools operating in the county.

Silver Township #9 has been preserved as a museum on the grounds of the Grand Meadow Heritage Center. An annual heritage festival is held at the center each September. Three other historic buildings are housed at this center which is located on L36 between Marcus and Correctionville. School groups visit the center and spend time at the school in the spring.

Another school was rescued in 1977 when Walter Voge, a Galva farmer who formerly attended a country school, purchased Center Schoolhouse #5 located in Diamond Township for $200. Voge moved the school to his farmstead and worked for more than 15 years restoring and maintaining the school.

He had purchased items from a sale of another country school several years earlier which he used to equip the school. Other people in the area donated items they had collected to help Voge furnish his school. The flag pole in front of the school, which was originally a gas street lamp, was donated by the City of Galva.

People from more than 20 states have visited the school, which is located in the northeast corner of Cherokee County, 6 miles north of Galva. People can make an appointment to see the school by contacting Voge at 712-282-4423.

Two schools are now being used as American Legion Halls. They include Cherokee #2 in Larrabee and Willow #4 in Quimby.

Two other schools have been maintained as township meeting centers and continue to be used as polling places—Rock #5 and Tilden #5.

Liberty #6 has been converted to a cabin located by a farm pond east of Larrabee.

Some 18 other schools have been recycled as farm buildings, six have been converted to homes, three are being used as garages, and three are vacant.

*Compiled by
Pat Behrens, Lois Grigsby,
Mildred Stevenson, and
Linda Burkhart with
information from the
Cherokee Historical Society
and the
Sanford Museum
117 E. Willow Street
Cherokee, Iowa 51012*

Grand meadow Heritage Center School in session

Tilden #5

Silver Township #8

Center School #5

101

Working with 1898, 1904, and 1915 atlas maps, members of the Chickasaw County Genealogical Society determined there were at least 98 schools in operation in the county at the turn of the century.

Members drove to each location in the spring of 1997 and found there were at least 41 country school buildings still standing.

Today those schools are being used in the following ways: 25 have been remodeled and are being used as homes; six are being used for storage; four are standing vacant; three have been restored and are operating as museums; one is used as an office; one is being operated as a school by the Mennonites; one is being used as a guest house.

Two of the schools have been relocated to the Bradford Village Museum near the Little Brown Church on the east edge of Nashua on Highway 346. Kraft School, or Bradford #6, is operated as a school for students in the spring of the year. The former Greenwood School is used to display antiques at this museum complex.

Another one-room school near Nashua, Maple Grove, has been remodeled into a two-bedroom cottage by two retired Cedar Falls teachers, Jim and Nancy LaRue.

Compiled by
Betty Tylee
805 East Main Street
New Hampton, Iowa 50659
and
Jeannette Kottke
2676 240th Street
Fredericksburg, Iowa 50630

Jacksonville #12 is restored as a school museum in Adolph Munson Park. The Jacksonville Historians Club gave the property to Chickasaw County and it is now maintained by the Chickasaw County Conservation Commission. Tomena Munson, president of the Jacksonville Historians Club, or secretary Cecelia Leuenberger will open by appointment for tours. Call 319-238-5661. The museum is located 3 1/2 miles north of New Hampton on Highway 63 and 4 1/2 miles east on a gravel road at 170th Street and Quinlan Avenue.

Maple Grove School   *Waterloo Courier Photo / Brandon Pollock*

Bradford #6—Kraft School

Jacksonville #9

New Hampton #8

Banner School

Research conducted by the Clarke County Historical Society and the Clarke Area Retired School Personnel Association during the winter of 1997 revealed that there were 34 former one-room country schools still standing in the county. In 1910 there were 108 one-room country schools operating in the county, according to a report, *The Four Trails and a Tale or Two,* produced by Margaret Reeve and Beverly Wilson.

Two of the schools are used as museums, and one is used as a community center and for reunions for those who attended the school.

Ten schools are vacant, nine have been converted to homes, four are used for storage, four as farm buildings, and four as garages.

Brush College #5 has been moved into Murray, located beside a log cabin as part of a historical complex.

Lipsett #8 has been relocated to the museum grounds on the south edge of Osceola on Highway 69. Museum hours are 2 to 5 p.m. on Wednesday, Saturday, and Sunday, May 1 through September 30.

Leslie #6 is used as a community center and for school reunions every two years. To reach the school, take I-35 south of Osceola 5 miles to the H45 exit (Elk Street) and go west on the paved road 1/2 mile where it bends south. Continue south for 2 miles to H48 (Doyle Street).

Compiled by
Mary Gardner
and
Effie Crawford
310 McLane
Osceola, Iowa 50213

Looking Ahead

"Many changes have occurred in the educational process. Now that we are out of the rural school era in Iowa, we sometimes look back to those times and think that if we could return to those educational practices our educational ills would be cured. However, it is a little like using a Model T in the automotive society of today. We cherish the thought of the past but turn to the future to solve the educational problems of today."—Margaret Reeve from *The Four Trails and a Tale or Two,* a booklet about the Leslie School in Clarke County.

Brush College

Lipsett #8

During the past 57 years the number of one-room school buildings in Clay County has declined from 59 in 1940 to an estimated 41 in 1997.

Two schools have been preserved as museums. The Rock Forest School, Peterson #4, has been moved into a museum complex in Peterson that includes a building with antique farm machinery and the first house built in Clay County. Country school classes are conducted for area students in the spring.

The Sunnybrook School was moved from Waterford Township to the park in Everly. The school can be visited by obtaining a key from city hall or the Everly library or by making an appointment with Shirley Steffen by calling 712-834-2400.

Two schools are used as township polling places. They include Logan Center in Logan Township and the Douglas Township School.

A school from Riverton Township has been moved to the Clay County Fairgrounds in Spencer where it is used as a health educational center. Another building in Gillet Grove Township is used as a rural maintenance garage.

Compiled by
Marilyn Meyer
2775 150th Avenue
Everly, Iowa 51338
with assistance from
Wayne Simington and
Dale Kabrick

Three schools are located side-by-side in Royal on the Clay Central-Everly school grounds. Two of the schools have been converted to homes and the other is used by the school for storage.

There are 23 schools that have been converted to homes. Seven are being used as farm shops or garages. Another building has been converted to a collection agency office in Spencer.

Clay County   *Photo by Jack Grandgeorge*

Riverton Township

Logan Center—polling center

Peterson #4—Rock Forest School

Sunnybrook School

Clayton County is the country school capital of Iowa. A team of members of the Genealogical Society of Clayton County, headed by Myra Voss, identified 89 one-room country schools in the county that are still standing. That is the most schools found in any Iowa county during the fall of 1996 and spring of 1997. It is probably the most that can be found in any one county in America.

Some 32 of the schools have been converted to homes, 15 are being used as farm buildings, 11 are used for storage, eight are used as polling places, four have been converted to garages, two are being used as workshops, and six are vacant.

At one time there were 181 one-room country schools in use in the county.

Some of the more unusual ways Clayton County country schools are being used today include:

- a tourist center in front of Spook Cave in Giard Township
- an antique mall in Marquette
- a supper club called Kountry Manor located near Farmersburg
- a craft shop in Littleport
- radio station KADR on Highway 128 near Elkader
- a funeral home garage in Lodomillo Township
- a town library in Littleport
- another school jointly owned and used by the American Legion and Amvets also sees duty as a town hall and polling place in Millville Township.

A restored one-room school house that dates back to 1866 has been relocated to the Froelich Museum in Froelich located 4 miles southeast of Monona on Highways 18 & 52. That school includes writing on the blackboard from 1906, original furnishings, and the original bell that visitors are invited to ring. The complex includes a general store and a replica of a working model of the tractor invented by John Froelich, which was the forerunner of the John Deere tractor. The store and school are open from Memorial Day to Labor Day, 9 a.m. to 5 p.m. except Wednesdays and Thursdays.

Another frontier village museum operated by the Clayton County Conservation Center and located at Osborne, 6 miles south of Elkader on Highway 13, also contains a restored one-room country school.

Compiled by
Myra Voss
712 Woodland Drive NW
Elkader, Iowa 52043

The other museum site with a country school—Musfeld #1—is the Plagmans Barn Museum located 2 miles east of Garber.

Clayton Center

KDAR—formerly Clayton Center

Froelich School Museum

Clayton School in use 1860 - 1963

Boardman #6

Compiled by
Ann Soenksen
2503 340th Avenue
DeWitt, Iowa 52742

In 1938 research done by the Clinton County Historical Society revealed that there were 133 one-room country schools and 14 town schools in operation.

Today at least 23 schools remain in the county. Fourteen have been converted to homes, three are being used for storage on farms, three others are vacant, one is used as a garage, and one is being used as a farm shop.

Another school, Flannery, has been relocated to the Soaring Eagles Nature Center on the edge of Eagle Point Park on the north side of Clinton. Discussions are underway with community groups to see if the school can be restored and opened for visitors and use by teachers.

Elk River #3, 1893

Elk River #3, now restored in Jackson County.

Flannery School

Sherman School

country school mailbox

Plugtown School

Three one-room country schools were saved and preserved as museums in the county by former teachers. They include the Little Red Schoolhouse, located 5 miles south of Denison on U.S. 59. This school was restored by Ramona Laubscher and opened in June of 1996 in conjunction with the Iowa Sesquicentennial observance.

Classes are held for students, and an old-fashioned Christmas program is held at the school the first Friday in December. An all-school reunion is being planned for former students and teachers of this school, formerly known as Soldier #4.

Included in this school is a pot bellied stove, black chalkboard, slates, Victrola, recitation bench, suspended globe, old school desks, kerosene lamps, water pail and cooler, drinking dipper, wash basin, old dinner pails, roller-type map case, sandbox, 48-star flag, hand bell, and much, much more.

This school is open by appointment by contacting the Laubschers at 712-263-5329.

Another school was preserved by teacher Hortance Pautch. Following her death, this school was relocated to a museum area in Dow City. Included at this complex is a railroad caboose and log cabin.

A third school has been restored by Collette Huntley who now teaches at the Denison Middle School. This school is located on a farm 1 mile west of Westside on the south side of Highway 30.

The East Boyer country school had its reputation sullied. After it closed, it was reportedly used as a "house of ill repute" for a time. It now stands vacant, equipped with a TV antenna but no bell tower.

Other schools have been converted to homes in Kiron and Goodrich Townships and another building is vacant.

Compiled by
Joel Franken
608 N. Main Street
Denison, Iowa 51442

Little Red Schoolhouse

Goodrich Township

Dow City Museum

East Boyer School

Westside Township

The only hotel in Iowa that has a room remodeled into a country school design is based in Perry. The recently renovated Hotel Pattee includes a sleeping room with a desk from a country school and a wallpaper border that features schoolbooks and the alphabet. Each room in the hotel is designed to reflect a different theme important to Perry's history.

The Alton School, which was in use from 1867-1961, is now preserved as part of the Forest Park Museum complex located at 1477 K Avenue in Perry. The museum is open May 1 through October 31, Monday - Saturday, 9 a.m. - 4:30 p.m., and Sunday from 1 - 4:30 p.m. Classes are held for area students at Alton School in the spring.

In the early 1900s there were more than 140 one-room schools operating in the 13 townships of Dallas County. Area residents could identify two schools being used as farm buildings and one other that is vacant. Individuals have marked locations where schools once stood with special signs.

For the past 12 years, annual reunions for graduates of the Maple Grove School have been held in Yale.

Compiled by
Myles Hegstrom
1737 142nd Place
Perry, Iowa 50220

Alton School House

Alton School in session

Pilot Lake School site

Machine shed

Information has been verified for 30 former one-room country schools in Davis County. The breakdown for usage includes 14 converted to homes, four farm buildings, and seven are vacant.

Three former schools are used as township meeting halls and voting places. They include Prairie Mound, now located in the village of Savannah; Jefferson in the Monterey settlement; and Stiles.

Another former country school was used as a transportation garage for the Davis County School District. It is now being used for storage.

Compiled by
Dee Altheide
RR#2, Box 106
Bloomfield, Iowa 52537

Center #5 has been relocated to the Davis County Historical Museum complex in Bloomfield. A house, barn, and log cabin are included in this museum complex. The museum area is open for visitors from 1-4 p.m. on Saturdays from Memorial Day to Labor Day.

Center #5

Center School, Grove Township, 1921

Stiles School—polling center

A team headed by Mrs. Betty Redman identified 58 one-room country schools standing in Decatur County.

Most of those schools—26—have been converted to farm buildings and 14 former schools stand vacant. Another eight have been converted to homes and four are being used as garages. One is used as an Assembly of God church in Decatur City and another has been converted to a hunting lodge. Two of the schools—Diamond in Grand River Township and Morgan Center in Morgan Township—are used as community centers and polling places.

Spurrier School was moved to the Liberty Hall Historic Center at 1300 West Main Street in Lamoni. It has been restored as a historical school museum and is open Mondays through Saturdays, 10 a.m. to 4 p.m., February through December. The children of Joseph Smith III attended this school in the 1880s and 1890s.

Work is underway to create a museum from the Brick School which was constructed in 1866. For awhile, this building was used as a band room for the Grand Valley School District in Kellerton.

Compiled by
Mrs. Betty Redman
RR#1, Box 46
Van Wert, Iowa 50262

Morgan Center School, voting precinct

Brick School

Spurrier School

*Compiled by
Pat Hucker and members
of the Delaware County
Historical Society
P.O. Box 70
Hopkinton, Iowa 52237*

Sarah Gillespie Huftalen, a teacher at the Arbor Vitae Summit School near Oneida, gained national recognition for her efforts to beautify grounds outside country schools. Huftalen got students and their parents involved in turning barren ground into an arbor with a variety of trees, shrubs, and flowers.

Huftalen accomplished this transformation in Delaware County from 1904-1909 and then repeated the same process at the Norwich School in Tarkio Township in Page County. Her efforts demonstrated what could be done and encouraged others to beautify school grounds. A diary with pictures illustrating this work is on file at the State Historical Society offices in Iowa City.

Nine country schools identified in Delaware County include three vacant buildings, two homes, and two museum-type schools.

The Pleasant Hill Red Schoolhouse was used as a home for many years and then restored as a museum operated by the Delaware County Conservation Commission. It is located on Honey Creek Road, 5 miles north of Manchester.

Another school used as a museum is Milo #7. It is part of a nine-building historical complex located in Hopkinton near Highway 38.

Red School

Milo #7

Delaware County School in early 20th century
(from Huftalen Collection, Iowa State Historical Society)

Delaware County

Norwich School, Page County

121

The 20 one-room country schools still standing in Des Moines County include buildings constructed with brick, limestone, and wood.

The two schools still maintained as museums are both constructed with limestone.

Zion, built in 1846 and operated as a school until the mid-1960s, is maintained by the Des Moines County Conservation Board. Arrangements for viewing this school—which contains the original slate blackboard, pot-bellied stove, desks, and books—can be made by contacting the county conservation office at 319-753-8260.

The Prairie Grove School is furnished with school memorabilia and houses the original bell in the belfry. It is used for Prairie Grove Township activities and is located behind the cemetery at the northwest corner of Beaverdale Road and North Prairie Grove Road west of West Burlington.

Park School, located at 5911 S. Madison Avenue in Burlington, now serves double duty as a chiropractic office and toy production center in the basement.

The former Middletown School has been converted to the Willow Branch Antique Shop. It is located on the south side of Highway 61 in Middletown.

Other uses for Des Moines County country schools include: two storage buildings, one farm building, seven homes, and six buildings are standing vacant.

Compiled by
Doretta Watson
7432 260th Street
Mediapolis, Iowa 52637
with assistance from
Mr. L.W. Mathews
of Burlington

Zion School in use

Zion School historical site

Nine country schools have been identified in Dickinson County in the spring of 1997. In 1911 there were 76 schools in the county, according to a plat map.

Lakeville #5 was moved to the University of Iowa Lakeside Laboratory near Milford for use as a library. In 1988, an addition was built on the east end of the structure which makes it appear as if two school buildings had been put together.

Westport Township Center School, which was used as a community center from 1955-88, was moved to Kenue Park. The school is being developed as a museum building as part of a historical park. The park is located 1/2 mile west of Highway 71 on 170th Street.

Richland #4 has been converted to a Seventh Day Adventist Church in Spirit Lake.

Four other buildings have been converted to homes. Another school has been converted to a storage building for a construction firm, and another school is vacant.

Compiled by
Margaret Gerdeman
P.O. Box 525
Okoboji, Iowa 51355

Westport Center

Richland #4

Residence in Milford

Lakeville #5

At least 22 schools are still in existence in Dubuque County and three are being used as museums.

Jefferson #5 is now owned by a doctor and used as a hunting lodge. Eight others have been converted to homes, seven are vacant, and three are used as farm buildings.

The museum schools include:

• Oak Grove School on 2nd Avenue, one block south of Highway 20 in Cascade. This restored building includes some of the original desks and the original blackboard. The school is open Sunday afternoons, May through November. It is part of a museum complex.

• Humke School has been restored, furnished, and relocated to the grounds of the Ham House Museum, 2241 Lincoln Avenue in Dubuque. The museum area is open from Memorial Day to Labor Day.

• Olberding School is now maintained in its original condition on a farm. It is located on Digman Road, 11 1/2 miles southeast of Dyersville.

Compiled by
Ruth Lansing
13307 Black Hills Road
Dyersville, Iowa 52040

Jefferson #5

Flannagen School

Olberding School

Kemp School

Compiled by
Mildred Bryan
4661 190th Street
Estherville, Iowa 51334

Nine former country schools were identified in Emmet County. Two have been converted to homes, two are vacant, and four are being used as farm buildings.

The former Bolstead School has been relocated to the Emmet County Museum at 1720 3rd Avenue South in Estherville. The museum complex is open on weekends. School classes sometimes visit the school.

Bolstead School   *Photo by Estherville Daily News*

Bolstead School

12 Mile Lake Center—now hog house

Denmark #6—home in Ringsted

Some 76 of the 175 one-room schools that once existed in Fayette County are still standing.

Most of the schools have been converted to homes—31. Some 14 schools are being used for storage, eight are vacant, eight have been converted to garages, six are being used as farm buildings, three are in use as township/community centers, and two are being used as churches. One school is used as a feed store.

Three schools are maintained as museums. They include:

• Dover #6—located at 7281 Great River Road near Clermont, open by appointment by contacting Donna Seitz, 319-423-7179 or 423-7200.

• Union #5—was developed into a "living interpretive center" during the U.S. Bicentennial observance. It is located on the Fayette County Fairgrounds on South Vine Street in West Union. Open during the Fayette County Fair the second week in July and by contacting the Fayette County Historical Center, Monday through Friday, 10 a.m. - 4 p.m., 319-422-5797.

• Center #6—located on a historical society complex in Waucoma, open by appointment by contacting Elaine Perry, 319-776-6441.

During the winter months of the 1951-52 school year, the County Superintendent of Schools visited each one-room school and took slides. A complete set of those slides is on file with the Fayette County Helpers Club and Historical Society. Prints of some of those slides have been used to illustrate the Nancy Barry article in this book.

Compiled by
Frances Graham
Fayette County
Historical Society
100 N. Walnut Street
West Union, Iowa 52175

Dover #6

Union #5 at fairgrounds

Union #5 on the move.

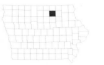

Working from an 1893 plat map, John Sebern determined there were 111 country schools operating in Floyd County that year. In the spring of 1997, Sebern traveled more than 300 miles and visited each of the 1893 school sites to determine that 19 schools were still standing on their original locations and four had been moved to new locations.

Sebern research revealed that three schools were being used as township halls and polling places, two were being used as farm storage buildings, and one is used as a museum opened during the Steam Engine Grain Harvesting Festival held Labor Day weekend.

Twelve schools have been converted to homes including nine tile brick buildings constructed in the 1930s.

One school is operated as a school for Mennonite children.

Locations/directions for some of these schools are listed below:

Cedar #2—used as a school for the Mennonites, is located approximately 7 miles north of Charles City, near the intersection of 110th Street and Shadow Road.

Scott Township #3—used as township hall and polling place, is 5 miles west of Marble Rock on Highway B60.

Ulster #1—operated as township hall and polling place, is 5 miles east of Rockford and 3/4 mile north on Jersey.

Pleasant Grove #6—now operated as the Bible Truth Hall church; located 8 miles south of Charles City on Shadow Road or T64, 1 mile on 300th Street, and then south on Rampart Street.

Ulster #3—is open as a museum in conjunction with the annual Steam Engine Grain Harvesting Festival held Labor Day weekend. It is located 7 miles west of Charles City on Highway 14 near the intersection of T38.

Compiled by
John Sebern
918 8th Street
Charles City, Iowa 50616

Pleasant Grove #1—built in 1858 and known as the "Little Red Schoolhouse," was moved to the Iowa State experimental farm and is used as a visitor center; located 1 mile south of Nashua and 3/4 mile west on 290th Street.

Pleasant Grove #6

St. Charles #12

Vacant building

Pleasant Grove #6

Scott #3

A country school that had been used as a farm building for 75 years was moved in April 1997 to the Franklin County Fairgrounds in Hampton, and work is underway to refurbish the school so that it can be used to give people an idea of what education was like in country schools.

The renovation of Fairview School is headed by Hampton teacher David Harms and is being supported by the three local education associations in the county. The school was donated by the Lovin family of rural Hampton.

Another country school located on the fairgrounds in the Pleasant Hill village complex is used as a craft shop during the fair. The fairgrounds are located on the west edge of Hampton along Highway 3.

A two-story stone structure school—Maysville—is listed on the National Register of Historic Places. In its early days, the building was used as both a school and church, with church services held on the second floor. Today the school is used as a polling place and is open for visitors on request. The contact person is Ken Showalter of Hampton, 515-456-2959. The school can be seen from Highway 65, 6 miles south of Hampton, east on 110th Street.

Wisner #5 is used as a township polling place for both Wisner and Richland Townships. School children visit the school in the spring. It is located 3 miles south of Meservey and 2 miles east on 230th Street.

Another school, Lee #5, is used as a township meeting hall and by fifth-grade classes from Iowa Falls. It is located at 50th Street and Juniper, north of Iowa Falls. The contact person is Verlynn Mensing, 515-648-2976.

Two other schools in the county—Bradford and Richland Center—are vacant.

Compiled by
Mrs. Milo Greiman
P.O. Box 415
Chapin, Iowa 50427

Rice School

Fairview School on the move.

Maysville School

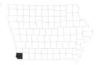

In Fremont County there are an estimated 14 one-room country schools still in existence. Historical records reveal that there were 110 rural schools operating in the county in 1910.

A project is now underway by the Fremont County Historical Society to put a sign at each location where a country school once stood.

Sunnyside School is preserved as a museum located in Sidney at the historical society grounds. The bell from Manti School is also located at the museum.

In 1990, voters in Green Township were polled about the future of the Hunter School which was then used as a polling site. Voters said they would prefer to vote in Tabor, but wanted to preserve the Hunter Schoolhouse as a historical landmark. The Harvard School was also maintained as a historical landmark by Mildred Doyle.

The Eastport School was moved to Payne and is now used as a scale house for a grain company.

Lots of schools have been converted to homes, but the Fairfield School was moved into Sidney and a two-story home was built around it.

Five other schools are being used as farm buildings, four are vacant, and a school in Farragut is being used for antique storage.

Compiled by
Winifred Rhoades
Box 337
Sidney, Iowa 51652
and
Lotus L. Foster
1203 Bluegrass Lane
Shenandoah, Iowa 51601

Fisher Center School

Fairfield School—Sidney, home built around it

Hunter School, Tabor   *Photo by Mike Whye*

Sunnyside School

Today in Greene County, 17 one-room country schools are in existence. According to an 1896 plat map there were 130 country schools operating in the county.

Usage for the schools includes four homes, three township polling places, a storage building, a garage, a farm building, and a museum.

Bristol #7 was moved to the Green County Fairgrounds in Jefferson where it is open for school during the county fair. The fairgrounds are located on the southeast side of Jefferson off Highway 30.

Votes are still cast at Cedar #5, Kendrick #5, and Willow #5. Highland #1 and #3 were moved into Churdan and converted to adjoining homes. In the past, when teachers first came to Churdan, they often rented these homes.

Rumor has it that ladies of the night utilized Dawson #4 after it ceased operation as a school. Today that school is used by the county as a storage building.

Compiled by
Joe Millard
5233 Panorama Drive
Panora, Iowa 50216

Dawson #4

Highland #1 & #3

Bristol #7

Willow #5

Some 62 former one-room country schools were identified in Grundy County in the spring of 1997. Over half of them—37—are being used as homes.

Other usage includes 14 farm buildings, four are vacant, and one is used for storage. Another school from outside the county was moved to Reinbeck and converted to a craft shop.

German #5, the last school to close in the county, is used as a township meeting and polling place.

Another school, Melrose #7, is used as an employee office building for the Green Products Company northeast of Conrad.

Perhaps Grundy County's most famous school, Colfax #9, has been converted to a museum and relocated to a park on Main Street in Grundy Center. The school is now known as the Herbert Quick School. It is named in honor of a former student who became a well-known Iowa author of 19 books and magazine articles.

Another school used as a museum is Colfax #3. It is located in the town of Morrison and is part of a multi-building museum complex maintained by the Grundy County Conservation Commission. Both of the museum schools are used by students from neighboring schools.

Compiled by
Nancy Hook
18419 205th Street
Grundy Center, Iowa 50638

Colfax #3

Colfax #9—Herbert Quick School

German Township #1

Melrose #7

Guthrie County has one of the highest number of country schools being used as voting centers in the state. Seven former one-room schools are now being used as township halls and polling places. They include Baker #5, Bear Grove #4, Grant #5, Jackson #2 (also known as Dale City School), Orange #5, Seeley #5, and Union #5.

Two other schools have been converted to homes, six are being used as farm buildings, four are vacant, and two have been restored as museums.

Baker #2 has been restored and relocated to the Guthrie County Fairgrounds which are located off Highway 44 west of Guthrie Center. The school is open for visitors to the county fair which is held Labor Day weekend. During the 1966 fair, former rural school teachers gave presentations recalling how country schools were operated.

Compiled by
Nona L. Hogge
103 3rd Avenue
Jamaica, Iowa 50128

Cass #7 was used as a farm granary before being restored and moved to the Guthrie County Historical Village museum complex located at 206 W. South Street in Panora. This complex is open from April 1 to October 15, Tuesday through Saturday 10-4 p.m., and Sunday 1-4 p.m.

Cass #7

Two one-room schools are operated as museums. Harmony Center has been moved to the Bonebright Museum Complex in Webster City at the corner of Superior and Ohio Streets. The school is maintained by the Hamilton County Historical Society. Tours are available by calling 515-832-2847.

Marion Center #4 is located in a beautiful but isolated area in the Bell's Mill County Park near the Boone River. The school is located on Bell's Mill Road approximately 6 miles northeast of Stratford. The school is maintained by the Hamilton County Conservation Commission, 515-832-9570.

Another well-maintained school, Liberty Center #5, is used as a township community center. This school is located 4 miles south of Blairsburg on U.S. Highway 69 and 250th Street.

Other country schools are located on the school grounds in Stratford and Jewell. Both are now used for storage.

Two others are vacant. Another school is used as part of a home, and another is used as a farm shop.

Compiled by
Larry G. Jansen
2711 260th Street
Kamrar, Iowa 50132

Harmony School in session   *Photo by Mike Whye*

Harmony Center School   Photo by Mike Whye

Liberty #5 is maintained as the only country school museum in Hancock County. The building was relocated to a park near a swimming pool at 220 West 6th Street in Kanawha. The school is open from 2-4 p.m. the first and third Saturdays and the second and fourth Sundays during the summer through the end of September. Student groups visit the school in the spring. The school contact person is Marge Larson, 515-762-3940.

Another school—Madison #6—has been converted to a gift shop. It is located at the Clark's Sawmill near the intersection of B16 and Highway 169 south of Forest City.

When Woden was consolidated with Crystal Lake, there was a classroom shortage so four country schools were moved to town and used as temporary learning centers. One of the temporary schools was retained for storage and two were converted to homes. The status of the fourth school is unknown.

Three other schools have been converted to homes, seven schools are vacant, and two are being used as farm buildings.

Compiled by
Imogene Schubert
679 2nd Street NW
Britt, Iowa 50423

Near Woden

Jamestown #8—made into hoghouse

Madison #6

Madison #5

Liberty School

*Compiled by
Bev Ryken
Ackley Heritage Center
Ackley, Iowa 50601*

At least 28 country schools were identified in Hardin County. The most common usages are nine homes and eight farm buildings; three garages, three for storage, and three are vacant.

Goose Creek #4 has been restored and is being used as a museum on the Hardin County Fairgrounds in Eldora. It is open during the fair and is maintained by the Eldora Historical Society.

Work was started in the spring of 1997 to restore the Clutterville School from Butler County as a museum. It is located in Heritage Park between Butler Street and Grundy Street in Ackley. Other buildings are being restored in this complex and include an 1870 home and a drugstore. Other planned additions are a windmill and a barn.

Goose Creek #4

McCoy School—couple restored building and maintain grounds

McCoy School restored

Clutterville School—1958 reunion

147

Some 24 schools have been identified in Harrison County by members of the Genealogical Society. Two of those schools are maintained as museums open for visitors. Classes are conducted for students at each of these schools.

The West Boyer Valley School, which was in operation from 1860-1959, has been relocated to the Harrison County Historical Village and Welcome Center. More than 10,000 items housed in nine buildings are included in the village which is open Monday - Saturday, 9 a.m. - 5 p.m., and Sunday from 12 - 5 p.m., from mid-April through mid-November.

The school is included as part of a self-guided tour for visitors. A teacher who taught at West Boyer—Dorothy Hirst—conducts classes for students in May. Two other school volunteers are former West Boyer students.

The Village and Welcome Center is located 5 miles east of Interstate 29 on Highway 30 near Missouri Valley.

The other museum school is Merry Brook, located at 211 Lincoln Way in Woodbine. When this school was closed, it was moved into Woodbine and used as a classroom and then for storage. In 1991, restoration was started to convert the school back to its original condition.

The museum is open on Thursday afternoons from 1:30 - 4:30 p.m. The county genealogical society meets at that time in the school basement. Classes are held for students in the spring.

Compiled by
Linda Dickman
2810 190th Trail
Woodbine, Iowa 51579
and Kathy Dirks
Harrison Co. Welcome Center
2931 Monroe Avenue
Missouri Valley, Iowa 51555

Another school, Mt. Hope #3, is used as a voting center in Union Township. Nine schools have been converted to homes, six are used as farm buildings, three are used for garages, and three other buildings are vacant.

Research continues to identify the status of other schools that still may be in existence. In 1933, there were 121 one-room schools operating in the county.

Merry Brook School in session

Merry Brook School

West Boyer School in session

In 1889 there were 108 one-room country schools operating in Henry County. In 1960, there were no country schools in operation in the county; in 1997, 24 of those buildings remain in the county. Eleven have been converted to homes, four are being used as farm buildings, three are in use as township/community centers, and two are vacant.

The best-known and most utilized museum school in the county is Pleasant Lawn. Classes are conducted there for area school groups in the spring and during the summer. The school is located in what is now Snipe Run Village on the Old Threshers grounds near Mount Pleasant. The school is open during the Old Threshers Reunion. At that time spelling bees, sing-alongs, and other programs are presented.

Two other restored schools are also located at the Old Threshers complex. Colfax #8 is used as a quilting center during the annual Old Threshers Reunion. The Oak Ridge School—a log structure first constructed in the 1840s—was demolished in 1977 and moved to Mount Pleasant where it was reassembled and located in the Log Village on the Old Threshers grounds.

The other museum school, Lowell #2, was restored during the Bicentennial observance and is located in the village of Lowell near New London.

Compiled by
Donald Young
305 West Green Street
Mount Pleasant, Iowa 52641

Colfax #8

Eagle #2

Pleasant Lawn School in session.

Pleasant Lawn School in session.

One of Iowa's best known citizens—Dr. Norman Borlaug—valued the education he received in a one-room country school in Howard County. In August 1996 Dr. Borlaug returned to the farm where he was born and reflected on his one-room school experiences.

One of the important lessons learned at country school was the experience of associating with Norwegians and Bohemians. Borlaug told the *Cresco Times-Plain Dealer* newspaper: "I learned that different ethnic backgrounds are artificial. People are pretty much the same. The difficulty is in communications. If you can get past the communications problems, people are alike. That was one of the basic principles I learned in that one-room schoolhouse."

Borlaug's first school has been restored and is now located on the home farm a dozen miles south and west of Cresco on 200th Street. In 1970, he received the Nobel Peace Prize for his work on the development of new wheat varieties used in various third world countries.

Saratoga #4, known as the Buresh School, has been restored and is used by students in Riceville and Cresco. Students like their country school experiences; their only complaint is using the outside toilets.

Another school is located on the Howard County Fairgrounds and is open during the fair, usually the last week in August.

The former Jamestown #1 is now part of the clubhouse at the Riceville golf course.

Probably the most northern location for a one-room school in Iowa is in Oakdale township, 1/2 mile south of LeRoy, Minnesota, on Highway V10.

The Cedar Valley Retired School Personnel Association started developing a complete listing of all remaining one-room schools still standing in Howard County as this book was going to press. Their research revealed that in 1907, there were more than 90 country schools operating in the county. They estimate that at least 51 schools remain in the county today.

Compiled by
Mary J. Stark
7897 Dale Avenue
Riceville, Iowa 50466

Little Red Schoolhouse Museum, Cresco

Dr. Norman Borlaug at New Oregon #8.

Saratoga #4

Oakdale Township Center

Some 33 former one-room country schools remain in Humboldt County. In 1883, there were 79.

Most of the schools—24—are now being used as homes; five are used as farm buildings, two are vacant, and one is being used as an office for Lang Flowers, Third Avenue South in Humboldt.

In July 1997 another school, Weaver #7, was resting on blocks near the Gilmore City school, ready to be moved and converted into a home.

Compiled by
Ms. Marilyn Hundertmark
1409 Elmhurst
Humboldt, Iowa 50548

Willow School was donated to the Humboldt County Historical Society for development into a museum. This gift was made by a former student, Dr. Clifford Michelson. The building is now part of the Humboldt County Museum complex in Dakota City.

Three schools converted to homes near Dakota City

Weaver # 7

Norway # 7

Flower shop in Humboldt

One school has been preserved as a country school museum and two others are being utilized by the Battle Hill Museum of Natural History.

The museum school, Grant #5, is located in Moorehead Pioneer Park on the west edge of Ida Grove. Country school is held during September for area elementary students. The students experience classes in orthography, ciphering, penmanship, geography, spelling, and reading from McGuffey readers. Nursing home residents also spend an afternoon in the school doing these subjects.

This school can be seen by contacting Harold Woolridge at 712-364-3579.

Two former country schools—Moorehead and Maple #5—are used to display stuffed wildlife at the Battle Hill Museum in Battle Creek. The museum collection includes more than 200 animals, 40 head mounts, and 100 hides and rugs. The museum is open on Sunday afternoons during the summer and other times by contacting Dennis Laughlin at 712-365-4576.

Three other schools have been converted to homes, one is used as a 4-H meeting place, another serves as a township meeting center, and there is one vacant building.

An oral history video that includes comments from 23 former country school teachers, and a companion book that recounts country school experiences by former country school students and teachers have been produced.

The book and video can be obtained from Conley Wolterman.

Compiled by
Conley Wolterman
501 Zobel Lane
Ida Grove, Iowa 51445

Garfield #4

Interior Grant # 5

Country School as Heritage Days float

In 1908, there were 135 one-room schools operating in Iowa County. Today, nearly half of those schools—65—have been located and are used in some way.

The Gritter Creek School is preserved as a museum by the Iowa Historical Society. The school was built with bricks produced locally and was in operation from 1874-1951. In the spring, Iowa history students from area schools take field trips to the school and classes are conducted the way they were years ago. The school is located 3 miles west of North English and 1/2 mile west of V52.

The Oak Grove School in Sumner Township is maintained as a tribute to a former teacher, Mary Voghtman.

Some 18 former one-room schools have been converted to homes and 15 are being used as farm buildings including seven machine sheds, six hog buildings, a chicken house, and a barn. Six are still used as township polling places, and five schools are vacant and remain at their original locations.

Another school has been converted to an antique shop near Williamsburg and the North Pilot School is being used as an antique shop at the Little Amana exit off Interstate 80.

Compiled by
Twila Gerard
P.O. Box 134
Millersburg, Iowa 52308
and
Netha M. Meyer
P.O. Box 741
Williamsburg, Iowa 52361

Pilot Grove # 6

North Pilot School

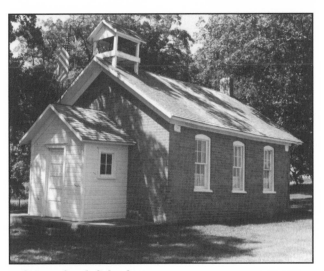

Gritter Creek School.

Oak Grove School

159

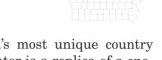

Iowa's only island city—Sabula—features Iowa's most unique country school facility. The Jackson County Welcome Center is a replica of a one-room schoolhouse that serves as an information center to visitors year-round.

The first floor of the center features authentic country school furnishings including student desks, a pot-bellied stove, blackboards, and a dunce cap. Visitors are encouraged to pull the rope that rings an authentic 330-pound school bell.

In the basement of the country school/welcome center is a modern gift shop that features local products. The second floor of the complex includes a modern conference room, kitchenette, and the director's office.

A picnic area and playground surrounds the school which is located at the intersection of Highways 67 and 52 west of Sabula.

Jackson County once had 147 schools. A review completed in July of 1997 identified 35 schools still remaining.

Two of the schools are listed on the National Register of Historic Places. They include Canton, one of the best examples of limestone school construction remaining in Iowa, and one of the oldest. It has limestone lintels across the tops of the windows; round, arched windows; and concrete heel molds. The front is made of concrete blocks. It was built in 1877 and is now maintained by the Jackson County Conservation Commission. It is located on the south edge of Canton.

The Millroeb School is the other National Register school. It was restored in 1995 with individual contributions and Resources Enhancement and Protection (REAP) funding. The roof was replaced and the school was made handicapped accessible. Students are able to spend a full day at Millrock learning from books that date back to 1839. The school is also maintained by the Conservation Commission. It is located south of Baldwin on 59th Avenue.

Elk River #3 is another school that was restored as a museum facility. It was moved to the Great River Threshers grounds in Miles where it is maintained as a museum and used in conjunction with the annual threshers event in July.

Two other schools are used as township meeting centers and Butler #2 is used as a township polling place. Wycoff is an American Legion meeting place in Miles.

Ten other schools have been converted to homes, and 15 are used for storage or farm use.

Compiled by
Janet Stange
6366 Highway 62
Maquoketa, Iowa 52060

Welcome Center

West Iron Hill

Canton School

161

*Compiled by
Judith A. Parsons
P.O. Box 173
Kellogg, Iowa 50135
and Hans J. Brosig,
Jasper County Museum
Box 834
Newton, Iowa 50208*

Early plat maps from Jasper County show that at one time there were 176 schools operating in the county in 1887. Today at least 42 former country schools remain, including one museum.

The museum school—Rock Creek #7—was relocated to the Kellogg Historical Museum complex in Kellogg. Seven museum buildings are housed at this site. They include a bank, church, hotel, a two-story barn full of farm-related tools and machines, and the One-Minute Midwest Manufacturing factory which is still producing parts for cars. The school was moved seven miles to Kellogg in 1989. Items from area country schools were collected and are housed in this building.

The museum complex is in Kellogg 2 miles north of Interstate 80 off exit 173. Hours for the museum are Monday through Friday, 9 a.m. - 4 p.m., Memorial Day through Labor Day and Sundays during that time period from 1:30 - 5 p.m.

A two-room school was constructed near Killduff in 1922 and continued to operate until it became part of the Lynnville-Sully School District in 1956. Today that building is used as the Richland Grange Hall.

Some 29 former schools have been converted to homes, seven are used as farm buildings, one is vacant, and one is being used for storage.

Rock Creek # 7

Killduff School —now Grange Hall

Fairview School

Forbes School

How the Jefferson County one-room schools were recycled is the title of a photo directory of former and remaining one-room schools in Jefferson County. Most of the schools included in the directory are still standing.

Three of the schools continue to be maintained much like they were at the turn of the century. Classes are held for elementary students at each of these schools.

Victory #8, located in Lockridge Township, is the most-used school. School reunions are held and family groups meet at the school. The school is located 1 1/2 miles north and east of Lockridge on H28.

Another restored school is Wooster or Peach Blossom. This school was relocated to Round Prairie Recreation Park approximately 9 miles southeast of Fairfield.

Elm Grove, or Center #4, has been preserved and relocated to the Jefferson County Fairgounds west of Fairfield on Highway 34.

Two country schools were moved to the Fairfield High School grounds and combined to be used as a school supply storage building.

Other usages for the Jefferson County one-room schools include 24 farm buildings, ten homes, four garages, four storage buildings, one machine shop, and ten buildings are vacant.

Compiled by
Lillian Thada
205 East Hempstead
Fairfield, Iowa 52556

Elm Grove # 4

Peach Blossom

Victory School

165

A 1981 research project revealed that 49 of the 222 one-room schools that once operated in Johnson County were still standing. A follow-up check in half of the townships done in September 1997 by Victoria Lock, who conducted the 1981 study, identified 14 schools still remaining.

Two of the schools continue to be preserved as museums. The old Coralville School, which was operated as a two-story, two-room brick facility from 1876-1950, is now called the Heritage Museum of Johnson County. The first floor is maintained as a turn-of-the-century classroom, and the second floor houses the offices of the Johnson County Historical Society.

The facility is open Wednesday through Saturday from 1 - 5 p.m., and on Sundays from 1 - 4 p.m. Group tours can be scheduled by calling 319-351-5738. The museum is located 1 mile south and 3 blocks west of Exit 242 off Interstate 80 in Coralville.

Another museum school is the Stone Academy located 2 miles north of Solon on Highway 1. This school began operating in 1842, five years before Iowa became a state, and continued to operate as a country school until 1953.

The old Stone Academy was located on the stagecoach route from Dubuque to Iowa City. It was constructed with blocks of coarse yellow limestone from the McCune Quarry off the Cedar River. A severe windstorm in 1978 lifted the roof off the building and some of the upper stones from the walls.

The Stone Academy Foundation was then formed to restore the building and develop the school to its original state. A renovation dedication was held November 13, 1988. The school is now furnished with 12 double-student desks; a round, iron, wood-burning stove; maps; and books. Classes are conducted at the school for students from Solon and Iowa City.

Two schools located in Cedar and Washington Townships are used as community centers and for voting. Six others have been converted to homes, two are used as farm buildings, and two are vacant.

Compiled by
Victoria Lock , Johnson
County Historical Society,
and Ed and Rose Ulch,
1160 Highway 1 NE,
Solon, Iowa 52333

Cedar Township

Coralville School now Heritage Museum.

Stone Academy interior.

Stone Academy

167

When Grant Wood was a young boy, each day as he meandered from his farm home to school, he observed the wonders around him—the plowed fields, the growing corn, the people, and the little country school he attended, called Antioch.

These scenes made a lasting impression on Wood, who immortalized them in such paintings as *Young Corn, Fall Plowing, Spring Turning, Dinner for Threshers,* and *Arbor Day*. These paintings established one of America's best-known regional artists.

Today, the school he attended from 1897-1901 is maintained as a turn-of-the-century museum by the Anamosa Paint 'n Palette Club. A special open house and art show is held at Antioch the last Sunday in July. The school is also open on Sunday afternoons from Memorial Day to mid-October. It is located 4 miles east of Anamosa on Highway 64.

The Old Sutton School has been relocated to the Jones County Historical Site. That complex also includes a library, church, doctor's office, and railroad depot. The site is open for visitors on Sunday afternoons from Memorial Day to mid-October. The main building at the complex houses teacher record books from most of the country schools in the county. The historical site is located near the Jones County Home, 2 miles east of Amber on E23.

The Hardscrabble School, Castle Grove #9, is the third museum school maintained as a museum in the county. The school began operating in the early 1870s when there were more Indian students than white students. The school operated until 1959. Many of the original furnishings have remained at the school. The first annual reunion for former students, teachers, and friends of the school was held in 1992. Classes are held for area students in the spring. Area groups meet at the school and the school is open for visitation by appointment by contacting Mrs. Albert Merfeld at 319-465-3719. The school is located 7 miles west of Monticello on D62 and north 1 1/2 miles on a gravel road (225th Avenue).

The former Roller School, located 6 miles west of Monticello, has been restored and is located in a picnic area.

Schools moved into Fairview and Amber are used as village meeting centers. Wayne #8 is used as part of a church. It is located 5 miles south of Monticello and 1 mile east of Highway 151 on E23.

Fifteen other schools have been converted to homes, nine are being used as farm buildings, and two are vacant.

Compiled by
Mrs. Wilma Merfeld
24651 Highway 38N
Monticello, Iowa 52310

Antioch School attended by Grant Wood.

Hardscrabble School interior

Roller # 9

Richland # 4

Keokuk is the only county in America that has a pair of two-story country schools listed on the National Register of Historic Places.

Both schools operated traditional ungraded elementary programs. Hayesville #9 included a primary through grade four program on the first floor, and fifth through eighth grade on the top floor. Lancaster #1 ran first through fourth on the bottom floor, and five through eight on the second.

Both schools were built before the turn of the century and were in operation for more than 60 years. Both are frame construction. The two schools are about four miles apart. The Hayesville School is located 5 miles south of Sigourney on Highway 149 and 2 miles west on G48. The Lancaster School is 2 miles east of Hayesville on G48 and another mile east on a gravel road. Then go north 1 mile at the intersection to a paved road, V5G, and 1/2 mile east.

These schools are open on special occasions, including an annual picnic attended by former students. Both schools are in good repair and well maintained.

Another school, White Oak #5, is maintained as a museum by the Keokuk County Conservation Board. It is located in the Belva Deer Outdoor Nature park northeast of Sigourney. A wood fence designed to keep animals out, which was common at the turn of the century but now very rare, surrounds the school. An early log cabin school is also located near the White Oak School. Students attend classes at the school and spend time on the nature trails each spring.

Another school, Stoney Point, is used as a private hunting club. Six schools are vacant, five have been converted to homes, and the rest are used as farm buildings.

Black Hawk #5 and Polk #2 from Jefferson County were relocated to become part of a furniture store located on Highway 78 west of Richland.

Compiled by
Charles H. Brower
16600 250th Avenue
South English, Iowa 52335

White Oak #5

Hayesville School

Lancaster School

An auction house in Irvington. A butcher shop in Garfield Township. A country dog kennel in Portland Township. A town hall in Rake. A furniture store in Swea City. A Sunday school annex in Lotts Creek Township. And a snowmobile clubhouse in German Township. These are some of the ways one-room schools have been recycled in Kossuth County.

According to a 1913 atlas, there were 210 one-room schools operating in Iowa's largest and only double county. Research in 1997 in 24 of the 28 townships revealed that at least 49 one-room schools are still standing. Information on 20 others that had been torn down or destroyed was also verified.

One school was opened as a museum school in July 1997 following five years of restoration. Sherman #5 was moved from the country into LuVerne near the center of town by Jack Guy, phone 515-882-3303.

Another school is in the process of being restored on the farm of John and Mary Ree northeast of Burt. A bell tower was put back on the school, Portland #5, and it was first opened for public viewing in September 1997. Plans call for the school to be open during an annual "old fashion" celebration at the farm the last week in September. A teacher's desk and original blackboards remain in the school, which was built before 1895. Student desks used in other country schools and other furnishings are being added to the school which can be seen by contacting the Rees at 515-924-3384.

A special display area that includes items from various Kossuth County one-room schools is housed in the Kossuth Historical Museum. The building is located at 122 South Dodge Street and is open from 10 a.m. to 2 p.m., Monday through Friday.

Two schools from Fenton Township, #2 and #4, were relocated and combined to become the Lone Rock Legion Hall.

The first school site in the county was in Union Township in 1856. It was really a dug-out cave which is now called "Gopher College." The location was dedicated in 1937 and a plaque was placed there by the Daughters of the American Revolution.

Some 19 schools have been converted to homes, eight are being used for garages, six are used as farm buildings, and eight are vacant.

Compiled by
Helen S. Hamilton
6176 Ridgecrest Drive
N. Syracuse, New York 13212
(former resident of
Bancroft)

Central School, Riverdale Township

Grant Center # 5

Kossuth County Museum interior

Lotts Creek # 4

Education in Iowa began in Lee County in 1830 when Dr. Isaac Galland hired Barryman Jennings to teach eight students. Today, a replica of that log cabin school stands in a picnic area/park adjacent to the Mississippi River.

The quick impact of school consolidation on country schools is well illustrated in this county. In 1959, there were 41 one-room schools operating. Three years later, all had closed.

Many have returned to operation today as museums.

Brush College has country school classes conducted for area students. This building, which is located 5 miles north of Fort Madison on the Augusta blacktop, is listed on the National Register of Historic Places.

Viele School is part of the Fort Madison, Farmington & Western Railroad Museum complex located near Donnellson just off Highway 2 between U.S. 61 and U.S. 218. Included in the complex are a steam sawmill, Model T cars, and a train museum.

The two-story Franklin School includes a second-floor replica of an early schoolroom created during the Bicentennial observance. The bottom floor is used for township meetings.

Hickory Grove School is another museum school where third-grade classes from Keokuk take a one-day field trip to experience what school was like a century ago.

Compiled by
Irene Smith, former country
school teacher
Box 148
Montrose, Iowa 52639

Including vacant buildings, storage facilities, and former schools converted to homes, there are perhaps 80 country school buildings in the county. This estimate was arrived at through comparisons with early township records, actual observations, and conversations with owners and farm neighbors.

Hickory Grove School

Franklin School

Brush College

Galland School

Viele School interior

Approximately one-third of the one-room schools that were once in operation in Linn County are still standing. The majority of the remaining schools—35—have been converted to homes.

Other usages for the schools include a cabin retreat located along the Wapsipinicon River, a grange hall near Mt. Vernon, a community center and library in Ely, and a Knights of Columbus Hall in Cedar Rapids.

Three country schools have been relocated to the Ushers Ferry Historic Village north of Cedar Rapids. One school has been developed as a town hall and another is being developed into a grange hall. Classes are conducted in the Cherry Valley School for visiting school groups in the fall and spring. Some 28 buildings are located in the complex which is designed to give visitors a chance to discover what life was like in small-town Iowa at the turn of the century.

Ushers Ferry is open June - August from 1 - 4 p.m., Thursday - Sunday and on weekends from September - October, 1 - 4 p.m. A $2 admission fee is charged. You can reach Ushers Ferry by taking the 42nd Street Exit off Interstate 380 and going west on Edgewater Road to Seminole Valley Road and follow the signs. The Ushers Ferry phone number is 319-398-5104.

Another school used as a museum is Abbe Creek. It is located 1 mile west of Mt. Vernon on road E48. The school is maintained by the Linn County Conservation Board. The school is open on Sunday afternoons from 1-7 p.m. from June until mid-October.

Compiled by
Janet White
159 State Street
Central City, Iowa 52214

The Sardinia Country School has been relocated to historical property in Walker on Rowley Street.

The Beach School, located off the highway north of Mt. Vernon, was approved for listing on the National Register of Historic Places in 1983.

Abbe Creek

Cherry Valley School interior

Cherry Valley School

There are at least 18 former one-room country schools still standing in Louisa County in 1997. At one time, there were 94.

The former Hopewell School is now being used as a Muscatine Island grocery store.

Another—Old Clifton—has been moved to Columbus City where it is being used as a city hall.

The former Fredonia School is now being used as a church in Fredonia, located about 1 mile east of Columbus Junction.

The Shellbark School is used for neighborhood gatherings and a Columbus City Township meeting center.

An annual rural school picnic open to anyone who attended, taught, or has an interest in rural schools is held at the Virginia Grove school the second Sunday in August. This museum school is operated by the Louisa County Conservation Board. It is located in a park with nature trails south of Columbus City.

The Pleasant View Country School has been relocated to the Louisa County Historical Museum grounds in Wapello. It is open in conjunction with museum activities, including a fall festival held the third Saturday in September.

Six other schools are being used as farm buildings, four have been converted to homes, two are used as garages, and two are vacant.

Compiled by
Helen L. Clark
413 Main Street
Columbus Junction, Iowa
52738

Hopewell School

178

Old Clifton, City Hall in Columbus City

Shellbark School

Pleasant View—now museum

179

Former Iowa Governor Nathan Kendall never forgot the education he received at a one-room country school in Lucas County. In his 1921 inaugural address, Kendall made reference to his educational experiences at Washington #2 (Greenville) and his teacher, Miss Susan Day.

In a letter to his uncle Kendall said, "I shall never forget Susan Day. I deemed her discipline very unreasonable in those days because I think I was altogether incorrigible, but later reflection has convinced me that she was a remarkably able educator."

The school that Governor Kendall attended still stands in the county. It has been moved to Russell and is now being used as a home.

Ottercreek #2, known locally as "Puckerbrush," was the last operating public one-room school in the county. It has been restored with a number of original books, pictures, and desks collected from other schools in the county. It is used several times a year by grade-school children and is open for public visitation. Puckerbrush is located next to the Lucas County Museum on the west edge of Chariton at 17th and Court.

Another school with a unique design featuring a corner door has been restored and is part of the Hunter Brothers Tree Farm. The May School is open for public viewing and is used with Christmas tree promotions. The tree farm is located in Lincoln Township west of Chariton.

Several other schools are being used as farm buildings. Others have become the basis for a residence, but are hardly recognizable as schools now. An estimated 30 schools remain in the county.

Compiled by
Betty M. Cross
R#2, Box 132
Russell, Iowa 50238

Considerable research has been done on Lucas County rural schools. Pictures of most of the schools and lists of former country school teachers and students, plus a comprehensive paper done by J.C. Durham, is housed at the Lucas County Museum in Chariton.

The May School

Puckerbrush School

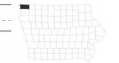

Some 23 former country schools are being used in a variety of ways in Lyon County.

Centennial #5 has been restored as an original country school museum and relocated to the Lake Pahoja campgrounds. The small home of a Lyon County pioneer teacher, Marie Medalen, has been located next to the school and work is underway to restore this building as an early 1900s home. The school is open for visitors on Sunday afternoons from Memorial Day through Labor Day. The school is staffed by members of the Lyon County Historical Society. Students have an opportunity to attend classes at this school in the spring. Lake Pahoja is located 6 miles north and 2 miles west of Inwood.

In 1981, two schoolhouses were moved to Little Rock and combined to create a funeral home. Another school was relocated to Inwood and used as a classroom, then converted to a library and is now used as a "Bridal to Blue Jeans" store.

Cleveland #8 is now being used as a shelter house in the park on South Main Street in Alvord.

Richland #4 is another school that has been used in a variety of ways. When it was closed it was used as a milk bottling business. It was then used for square dances and now has been converted to a home.

A family south of Larchwood is utilizing country schools for their home and garage.

Uses for other remaining one-room schools in the county include: four farm buildings, four homes, two garages, and five are vacant.

Major historical relationships of Lyon County country schools have been developed and maintained by Mrs. Leo Johnson of Inwood. She develops a pictorial display each year for the county fair.

Compiled by
Galen Jackson
908 South Tama Street
Rock Rapids, Iowa 51246
and Elvira A. Johnson
208 S. Maple
Inwood, Iowa 51240

Fair display, Lyon County

Cleveland # 8

Liberal # 8

Centennial # 5

In 1888, there were more than 130 country schools in Madison County. In 1997, at least nine still remain.

Three of those are used as museum schools and are open for public visitation. Two of the museum schools are located in the Madison County Historical Complex at 815 South 2nd Avenue in Winterset. They include a log school, restored to an authentic 1850's look, and the Tusha Country School, which was moved to the museum complex in 1991 from south of Winterset. In the spring, elementary students have the experience of returning to country school classes.

In addition to a beautiful limestone museum headquarters building, the complex includes a stone barn and stone privy, a log post office, law office, mercantile building, gas station, blacksmith shop, church, and agricultural buildings.

The historical complex is open to visitors from May 1 to October 31, 11 a.m. to 4 p.m. on weekdays and 1-5 p.m. on Sundays. The museum office is open year-round on weekdays from 9-4 p.m. Admission is charged.

Another significant school preserved in the county is the Bennett-North River Stone School, a limestone structure built in 1874. This building is listed on the National Register of Historic Places. It is located 4 miles north of Winterset and 1 1/2 miles east. Signs direct visitors. The school is open by appointment for groups during the Covered Bridge Festival in the fall.

Two other schools—Jefferson (9 miles north of Winterset on Highway 169 and west approximately 3 miles) and Webster Center (8 miles west of Winterset on Highway 92 and 3 miles south on P53)—are used as township centers and polling places. Both schools have remained at their original site locations.

The Penn Center School is used by 4-H clubs. It is located 5 miles south of Interstate 80 on P53.

One school is vacant, one has been converted to a home, and another is used as a farm building.

Compiled by
Wendell Spencer
Madison County
Historical Society
815 South 2nd Avenue
Winterset, Iowa 50273

Bennett—North River School

Tusha School in session

Penn Center School

Tusha School Sesquicentennial event

Some 33 country schools remain in Mahaska County. The usage for the schools in 1997 includes 14 homes, seven farm buildings, seven are vacant, three churches, one township polling place, and a museum.

The museum school is Prine—the oldest school in continuous use in the county. It was used as a school from 1861 to 1966. It was moved in 1967 to the Nelson Pioneer Farm, located northeast of Oskaloosa in Spring Creek Township. It is furnished with country school furnishings including a row of dinner pails on a shelf. The farm complex and school are open during the summer and during the annual Craft Day in September. Classes are held for school children and spelling bees are conducted for adults.

An overflow of students in the early 1900s caused two one-room schools to be built side-by-side in Evans Township. One was closed in 1924 and converted to a church. The other operated until 1962 and then was remodeled and is used as a home today. These buildings are located west of Oskaloosa on Highway 92 and then north on Galeston Avenue.

Center School in Jefferson Township is used as a polling place. It is located southwest of Oskaloosa on G71 or 330th Street on the way to Bussey.

Three country schools were moved into New Sharon by Dr. Bartlett and placed on land adjoining his home and office. These schools have been converted to homes.

Compiled by
Henrietta Groenenboom
225 Lincoln Avenue
Oskaloosa, Iowa 52577
and Patricia Patterson
1407 Edmundson Drive
Oskaloosa, Iowa 52577

Evans Township School

Prine School

West Center School

187

*Compiled by
Darlene J. Hodges
1504 Highway T15
Knoxville, Iowa 50138*

Fourteen former one-room country schools have been identified in Marion County. Five have been converted to homes, three are vacant, others are being used as farm buildings.

Names of some of the schools still standing include: Highland, Free, Liberty Corner, Pleasant Grove, Indiana, Spring Hill, Fairview, Victory, and Vigilance.

The Pleasant Grove School has been restored and equipped as an original country school. It is located at Marion County Park in Knoxville, along with several other restored buildings.

School northwest of Pella on Highway 163

Marion School—Otley

Pleasant Grove School

One country school is now operated as a museum in Marshalltown by the Marshall County Historical Society. The Weatherbee School Museum, also known as Taylor #4, is located at 50 North 2nd Avenue in Marshalltown. It can be visited by appointment by contacting the Society at 515-752-6664.

Five other schools have been converted to homes in Beaman, Green Mountain, LeGrande, and Marshalltown, and two buildings are vacant.

Compiled by
Marleen Meyers
1703 Laurel Drive
Marshalltown, Iowa 50158

Marleen Meyers, a retired teacher living in Marshalltown, took slides of many central Iowa one-room schools in 1975-76 and revisited many of those school locations to provide photos and information for this book. She was assisted by Marilyn Goeldner of Boone and Warren Terpstra of Sully.

Spring Valley

Taylor #4   *Photo by Mike Whye*

Timber Creek #4—no longer in existence

191

Mills: 6 Schools, 1 Museum

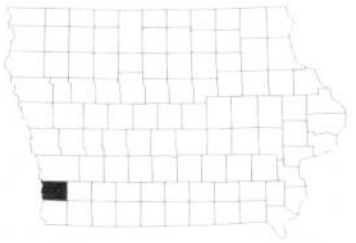

The former West Liberty #2 country school has been moved to the Mills County Historical Museum complex located east of the Glenwood City Square in Glenwood Lake Park. The school is furnished with books, desks, and other furnishings used at the turn of the century. Several buildings are located at the historical complex. They include a jail, barn, machinery hall, and the cottage of a pioneer family.

The museum complex also includes antique cars and tractors, a threshing machine, and a historical display of 4-H uniforms. The complex is open Saturdays and Sundays from 1:30 - 4 p.m., Memorial Day to Labor Day, and by appointment by calling 712-527-5038.

Another school, Golden Hill, is used by a gun club as a retreat center. It is located in Deer Creek Township.

Two other schools have been converted to homes, one is being used as a farm storage building, and another school is vacant.

Compiled by
Lester I. Hunt
305 East Cooledge Street
Glenwood, Iowa 51534

West Liberty #2

Mills Golden Hill

East Sunbeam—converted to home

Some 48 of the 95 schools that were once the pride of their townships are still serving residents in Mitchell County.

The buildings located in the summer of 1997 were being used in the following ways:
• 22 are standing as houses with 17 lived in now, three livable but currently vacant, and two used for storage
• 15 have been converted to farm buildings and one is being used as a garage
• two are being used for businesses

Lumber from six schools was salvaged to construct a cabin, corn crib, two apartment buildings, a farm shop, and a business. Three other schools were destroyed by fire and one was struck by lightning and burned to the ground while in use as a farm building. Two schools deteriorated from lack of maintenance.

Citizens in Mitchell County have preserved one school as a museum and are at work on restoring a second. Union #1 was moved to the Mitchell County Fairgrounds on Chestnut Street in Osage. It is open during the fair in July and can be visited by appointment by calling the Mitchell County Historical Society at 515-732-1269. Included with the school is an original outhouse and fencing around the yard. Area fourth graders attend classes there in the spring.

Renovation of Cedar #7 was undertaken in 1997 by former students, children of former students, and township residents. That school has remained on its original site since it opened in 1857. It is located at 3272 Foothill Avenue in the village of Morea. The school is open during special events in the area or by calling the historical society.

A school converted to a business is the Newburg School built in 1858. Virl Deal has converted this building to a barbershop called the Hairport. When Deal isn't cutting hair, he is building airplanes.

Burr Oak #5 now houses the Bullis Discount House on the east end of Osage at 1815 State Street. The interior contains the original wainscotting that was a standard feature of many one-room schools in Iowa.

Another schoolhouse is used as the party room for the Cedar Valley Supper Club located on Lancer Avenue on the south edge of Osage. Before being relocated to Osage, this school served as the depot for the "Star Clipper" railway in Traer.

Bert Decker, a local farmer, purchased Union #2 and cut seven feet off the bottom of the building so he could move it in two pieces without having to deal with power and telephone company lines. The top half was placed on a foundation and used for chickens. The bottom was positioned on a high cement foundation. A roof was put over it so it could be used as a hog house.

Compiled by
Everett and Jaceil Gisleson
2120 340th Street
Osage, Iowa 50461
and
Richard and Elanor Bower
811 Walnut
Osage, Iowa 50461

When the Decker farm was sold, Joseph Duren bought the top part of the school (the chicken house) and moved it 3 1/2 miles and converted it to a farm shop. In 1994, Duren's son, physically handicapped from birth, lost his home to a fire. The farm shop building was remodeled into an easily accessible home for Brian.

Two nationally-known figures attended country schools in the Mitchell County area. Author Hamlin Garland attended Burr Oak #3. Hamlin wrote about his country school experiences in Iowa and wrote several books including *A Daughter of the Middle Border* which received Pulitzer Prize recognition in 1922.

A nationally-known artist, Atlanta Constance Sampson, grew up near Toeterville on the Iowa-Minnesota border. Following a teaching career in Detroit, Sampson moved to New York where she devoted the rest of her life to painting.

Cedar Valley Supper Club

Newburg School—now barber shop

195

Compiled by
Keith Robinson
502 1/2 South 7th Street
Mapleton, Iowa 51034

Early records show that 117 one-room schools were operating in Monona County in 1906. In 1919, 94 were still operating and today there are at least 16 former one-room schools still standing.

Five have been converted to homes, five are used as farm buildings, and four are vacant.

Wilson #5 has been moved to the Monona County Fairgrounds in Monona and is being used as an office.

Franklin #7 has been moved to the Kiwanis Museum Complex in Onawa. Included at that site are an early depot, jail, church, log cabin, and a county historical building. The complex is open weekends from 1-4 p.m., Memorial Day to Labor Day. Events are held at the school for elementary students in the spring.

Franklin #7

Culver School

Center School

In 1911 there were 103 schools operating in Monroe County. At least 21 of those schools are still standing, including 16 at their original locations.

Two vacant schools north of Albia—Union Hall and Grays Greek—are being considered for development into a museum school by the county historical society.

The former Dry Ridge School has been relocated to the school building in Lovilla and is used as a school for Head Start students.

Another school has been converted to a church and two others have been attached to existing church buildings.

The school known as Pumpkin Center is used as a community center and polling place in Mantua Township located east of Albia.

Two other schools are used for storage, two others have been converted to farm buildings, and seven others are vacant.

Compiled by
Rosalie Mullinix
R#1
Albia, Iowa 52531

Cuba School

Pumpkin School

West Point School

197

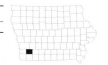

The Pittsburg School, typical of the more than 100 one-room schools operating in Montgomery County in the 1880s, has been preserved and is operated as a museum school by the Montgomery County Historical Society.

The school has been equipped with donations and furnishings from other Montgomery County schools. Retired teachers decorate the building for special activities throughout the year. Country school classes are conducted for elementary students.

The school is located on the Montgomery County Fairgrounds on North Fourth Street in Red Oak. The school is open during the county fair and at other times by appointment. The Pioneer Mutual Insurance Company was founded in this school in 1870.

Another school moved into the town of Stanton by the Stanton Historical Society may be developed and used as a museum school. It is located at the south end of the business district.

Nearly half of the remaining one-room schools in the county—16—have been converted to homes. Seven others are being used as farm buildings, six are vacant, and one is used as a garage.

Compiled by
Donald Peterson
Box 231
Stanton, Iowa 51573

Garfield #8 is now used as a Garfield Township community center. Pilot Grove #7 has been moved into Stanton where it is used as a chapel for the Evangelical Covenant Church.

Maplehurst School

Cramer Chapel School, Stanton Historical Society

Pittsburg School   *Photo by Jan Castle Renander, Red Oak Express*

At least 25 former one-room schools are still standing in Muscatine County.

Melpine #5 is located in Wildcat Den State Park and is operated as a museum building. It is located beside a former grist mill in the park. The school is staffed by volunteers on Sunday afternoons during the summer. Last spring more than 400 area students visited the school and were taught by former country school teachers. The park complex is located south of Highway 61 on Y26.

The former Walnut School is also being preserved as a school on the Swayze farm. It is located 1 mile east of the Highway 61 bypass and then 1 mile southwest on Old Burlington Road.

Former territorial Governor Robert Lucas once owned the Lucas Grove School. That school is now used as a farm building.

Thirteen other schools have been converted to homes, two others are used as farm buildings, and two are vacant. The former Cranston School is used as the Cedar Township community center and Clearview #2 is used as a Seventh Day Adventist Church in Muscatine.

Compiled by
John Deason
501 Fairview Avenue
Muscatine, Iowa 52761

Clearview #2

Geneva School   *Photo by John Deason*

Hazeldale #3   *Photo by John Deason*

Melpine #5   *Photo by John Deason*

The following statistical summary documents the life of the one-room country school in O'Brien County.

In 1896, 136 one-room schools enrolled 4,538 students. By 1953, the number of schools operating in the county had declined to 73 and by 1979, all one-room schools were closed.

In July of 1979, at least 23 schools were identified in the county. Fourteen were being used as homes. They were located in Sheldon, Archer, Primghar, Hartley, Matlock, and in the country.

The schools maintained as museums include Center #3 located in Heritage Park in Primghar, and Floyd #9, which was moved to 1423 Park Street in Sheldon.

Three other schools are used as garages, two are used as farm buildings, and three are vacant.

"I am certain that there are more schoolhouses still hidden on the many farmsteads in O'Brien County that I could not find, many are being used as farm buildings of some sort," Tuttle admitted.

Compiled by
Harold E. Tuttle
1129 11th Street
Sheldon, Iowa 51201

Floyd Township #9—today

Floyd Township #9—later Sheldon Independent School

Compiled by
Imy Tillotson
607 9th Avenue
Sibley, Iowa 51249

At least 25 one-room schools remain in Osceola County.

Most of the schools—20—are being used as farm buildings or for storage on farms. Four others have been converted to homes.

The former Goewey #5 school has been moved to the Osceola County Fairgrounds where it is open for visitors during the fair the third week in July. The fairgrounds are located on the west side of Sibley just off Main Street.

West Holman #5—Sibley

Goewey #5

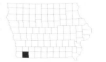

In conjunction with Iowa's Sesquicentennial observance, volunteers identified original locations for 143 rural schools that once stood in Page County. Markers that include the name of the school and the years it was open were placed at each of these locations.

In the summer of 1997, ten country schools remained at their original locations and 16 others have been relocated in the county. One of those schools—Goldenrod—has won national acclaim as one of the best one-room schools in America as a result of the work of teacher Jessie Field Shambaugh. Jessie began after-school groups called "Boys' Corn Clubs" and "Girls' Home Clubs," which developed into 3-H and finally the 4-H Club programs of today.

Goldenrod is listed on the National Register of Historic Places and is operated as a "working school" by members of the Nodaway Valley Historical Museum located in Clarinda at 1600 S. 16th Street. Many school classes visit for a morning of "one-room school" classes taught by museum staff members, many of whom were former country school teachers.

In the main museum complex, a separate area has been converted to a country school area that contains authentic furnishings from former Page County country schools. Notebooks for each township contain records, photos, and clippings about schools that once operated in the township. Both the Goldenrod School and the NVH Museum are open to visitors Tuesday through Sunday from 2-4 p.m., phone 712-542-3073.

Another comprehensive museum school—Morning Star—has been relocated to Sportsman's Park in Shenandoah north of Ferguson Road. It is open by appointment by contacting the Greater Shenandoah Museum at 712-246-1669.

Three other schools have been converted to antique shops. One is located just west of Braddy Park one block east of Highway 71 and Main Street in Braddyville. Two other schools, High Prairie and Science Ridge, have been moved for use by an antique dealer near Yorktown. From the Yorktown sign on Highway 2 go 1 1/2 miles west, then turn north on M56 for 2 miles where the main road turns west and becomes J32. Continue for 2 1/2 miles to the "antiques" sign on the north side of the road.

Compiled by
Elaine Christensen
Box 107
Blanchard, Iowa 51630

Two other schools are now being used as church facilities in Braddyville and Shambaugh. Another school can be easily seen from the Wabash Trail. Seven others are vacant, four have been converted to homes, two are being used for storage, and two are used as farm buildings.

Nishna Valley Museum

Goldenrod School   *©Taylor Pharmacy*

Goff School

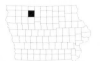

At least 15 one-room country schools are still in use in Palo Alto County. Most of the known remaining schools—seven—have been converted to homes. One of the schools is used as a summer home at Lost Island Lake. Six others have been moved into Ruthven. Two of those are located side-by-side on Washington Street.

Three schools are used as voting centers in the townships of Lost Island, Independence, and Great Oak.

Another school is used as a kennel and for storage on a farm. One is vacant and one is used for storage.

The only school restored as a museum is located in West Bend. West Bend #1 was built in 1872 and classes were held there until 1915. When schools were consolidated, that building was moved into town and used as a public school annex. It was restored to a turn-of-the-century school and dedicated as a museum in 1976.

Today the school is open Saturday and Sunday afternoons from Memorial Day through Labor Day. Many visitors come to recall their experiences as pupils in a one-room school. Teachers bring students for classes at the school in the spring. If the day is cool, a stove can be fired up.

Tours are available from May 1 through October by contacting Margaret Grimm, 4473 550th Avenue, West Bend, Iowa, 50597.

*Compiled by
Vickie Kesler
Palo Alto County
Genealogical Society
2018 10th Street,
Emmetsburg, Iowa 50536*

Highland #4—now in Ruthven

Independence Township

Lost Island Township—built by WPA 1939

West Bend #1

In 1890, the Plymouth County Superintendent of Schools reported there were 142 rural one-room schools operating in the county with an enrollment of more than 3,600 students.

Data compiled by Plymouth County Historical Museum staffers revealed at least 28 one-room schools are still standing in the county. This includes three buildings maintained as museums.

Three of the one-room schools are located on the Plymouth County Fairgrounds, 4th Avenue NE, in LeMars. One of those buildings, Elgin #2, is used as a country school. The other schools have been converted to a toy shop and a saloon where soft drinks are sold during the fair by the American Legion. All three buildings are open during the fair in late July. Area students attend the country school classes at Elgin #2 in the spring.

Garfield #1 is another school that has been restored and is maintained as an original country school. It is now located on the Kingsley-Pierson school grounds in Kingsley. Students studying Iowa history attend classes at the school. The school is also open on July 4th and during the Kingsley Augustfest celebration.

Another school preserved as a museum is located in the village of Struble on Highway 3 about 9 miles east of Akron. Surrounding the school is the original outhouse, a merry-go-round, flagpole, and underground cave used as a storm shelter. A 1900s country store and farm home are located near the school, which is open by contacting Mary Lamoureaux at 712-568-2696.

Elgin #8 is used as a community center in Struble. Three schools were moved to Kingsley and now stand side-by-side and are used as private residences. Other homes in Akron, LeMars, Merrill, and Craig are former country schools. All told, there are at least 12 schools in the county that have been converted to homes.

Five other schools have been converted to farm buildings, two are used for storage, two are garages, and three are vacant.

Compiled by
Delores Burkard and
Margaret Henrich
Plymouth County Museum
335 1st Avenue SW
LeMars, Iowa 51031

Hancock Township

Elgin #3—Struble

Stanton #5

Steel School

Plymouth County Fairgrounds

209

Some 39 one-room schools have been identified in Pocahontas County.

Two schools—Colfax #5 and Lincoln #5—have been moved to the Wiegert Prairie Farmstead. An annual fall festival is held there in mid-August. There are a variety of demonstrations including candle and rope-making, quilting, threshing, haying, and sheep shearing.

The Colfax School is used to display the crafts and Lincoln is used as a country school. Classes are held for area students at this school.

A pioneer church, a 1900s farmstead, and native prairie is maintained at this complex which is located near Palmer or 1 mile west of the intersection of C66 and N65.

The former Lizard #8 has been renamed "Country Charm" and is used as an artist's studio where floral displays are created. The studio is located 3 miles east of Palmer on Highway N65.

Roosevelt #7 has been moved to Streit Park in Rolfe where it is sometimes used as a park shelter house.

Four schools from Grant Township have been moved into Pocahontas and are now being used as homes.

Other schools have been converted to homes in Laurens and Havelock. All told, 18 schools have been converted to homes in the county. Fourteen former schools are being used as farm buildings, and three are being used as garages.

Compiled by
Audrey E. Simonson
25179 410th Street
Rolfe, Iowa 50581

Lincoln #5 interior

Lizard #8

Wiegert Prairie Farmstead   Photo by Pocahontas Co. Conservation Board

Work is underway to restore a one-room country school in West Des Moines. The old Bennett School was moved to a site beside Jordan Creek Elementary School during August of 1997. Work was soon started to restore the school to its original condition as a 1920s one-room school. Plans call for having West Des Moines students attend country school classes in the building which is now located on the campus of the new 9th grade school, Valley Southwoods on Fuller Road. The school is being restored by the West Des Moines Historical Society.

When this project is completed, there will be three country school museums in the county. The school at Living History Farms is actually a replica of a country school. It was built wider than normal to accommodate greater numbers at one time.

Another school on the state fairgrounds, North Lincoln, was relocated from Warren County in 1968. It was furnished and equipped by the Iowa Association of Classroom Teachers, a department of the ISEA.

The former brick Nagle School is now used as an office for Warren Transport Inc. located south of Ankeny at 1220 NW 78th Avenue.

The former Pleasant Corners School in Des Moines is now part of the Boys' & Girls' Club of Central Iowa, located off East 14th Street at 1350 E. Washington.

According to sources in the Saydel and Southeast Polk School Districts, at least seven other one-room schools have been converted to homes.

In 1939 there were 61 rural ungraded schools operating in the county. Included were 48 one-teacher schools, seven two-teacher schools, four three-teacher schools, one four-teacher school and one five-teacher school.

Compiled by
Bill Sherman
ISEA
4025 Tonawanda Drive
Des Moines, Iowa 50312

212

Sandridge School—Southeast Polk County

Nagle School

Bennett School

Living History Farms replica

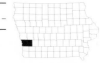

Adults from across America are now experiencing what it was like to attend a one-room country school in Iowa in the 1930s. The program, which was jointly developed by the Walnut Merchants Association and the Walnut Creek Historical Society, received rave reviews from a group of tour guides from Las Vegas in the spring of 1997.

Most of the classes at Monroe #8 are conducted by Lois Hansen, who taught in the school before it was closed. Participating adults who go back to school are given a student dossier sheet and are asked to assume that role. The adult students sit in assigned seats enabling their teacher to call them by their assumed name. A one-hour program has been developed for tour groups and a two-hour version is presented to Elderhostel participants. Programs are also held for student groups in the spring. For more information, contact the Walnut Welcome Center at 712-784-2100.

Last minute efforts to save another one-room country school in the county were successful in the summer of 1997. The future of Garner #3 was threatened when the Westfair Board asked the Council Bluffs Retired Teachers Association, owners of the school, to move the building to a new location to make way for new construction. The teachers lacked resources to move the school. Publicity about the problem by local media attracted the attention of Penny and Scott Wright. They agreed to move the school to Big Grove Country Inn, located near Oakland. Before the moving plans could be completed for the move, the Wrights learned that the stretch of Highway 6 between Council Bluffs and Oakland they needed to use was going to be closed most of the summer. The scheduled 27-mile trip was moved up and intervention by the Governor's office helped speed up the process for the necessary permits. The Wrights spent the summer painting and refurbishing the school, which was built in 1878. School furnishings collected by the retired teachers 20 years earlier remained with the school. The Wrights were able to open the school for visitors in the fall of 1997.

The Big Grove Country Inn and Hunting Lodge is located on Highway M37 east of Oakland. Plans are to add a church and other buildings to a pioneer cabin which is used as a hunting lodge and bed and breakfast facility.

Another school, Newtown #1, is maintained as a museum school where children attend classes. It is located in the Edgington Memorial Park, 1/2 mile east of Avoca on Highway 83. The park includes a picnic area, swimming pool, tennis courts, and ball diamonds. The school is open on Sunday afternoons from Memorial Day to Labor Day, and can be seen at other times by contacting Richard Day at 712-343-2309.

Pleasant #5, built by the WPA in 1939, continues to be used as a polling place in Pleasant Township. The school is located 3 miles west of Avoca on Highway 53 and 1 mile south on 410th Street. Valley #4 was moved into Hancock and is used as a Legion Hall. Valley #3 is used as a storage building. Three former one-room schools are located north of Highway 6 in an 8-mile area along road M37. Two of the schools are vacant and one is used as a farm building.

Compiled by
Bill Sherman
and Pat Rock
30589 430th Street
Avoca, Iowa 51521

214

Monroe #8

Monroe #8 in session

Compiled by
Frances E. Hall
1726 Spring Street
Grinnell, Iowa 50112

Malcom #6, which was operated as a one-room country school from 1879-1965, continues to serve students and others as a museum facility. The school is now part of the Heritage Park Museum located on the county fairgrounds on Highway 146 south of Grinnell.

Visitors are welcome at the museum site from May 1 to November 1. The school is open for students in the spring and during the county fair in late July. This building contains a collection of pictures of other county one-room schools, official school registers, and other historical information.

Three other schools in the county have been maintained and equipped with original items. Chester #9 is used as a meeting place for the Chester Grange. Grant #9 is a meeting place for the Baptist Church, and Scott #7 is used as a township polling place.

Other former schools have been remodeled into homes, converted to farm buildings, or are vacant.

Malcom #6   *Photo by Grinnell Herald-Register*

Chester #9

Malcom #6   *Photo by Grinnell Herald-Register*

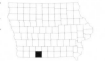

Some 37 former country schools remain in Ringgold County. Two have been preserved as museums.

In 1894, 130 schools were operating. By 1940, there were still 97 in use.

Monroe #8, or Jackson Hill, was built in the 1880s and used as a school until 1954. It was moved to a farm and used as a voting center and then for storage. In 1992, it was moved to the Ringgold County Fairgrounds and restored to a turn-of-the-century country school. The school is open during the county fair in July and students from area schools attend school in the fall and spring.

The Hazel Glen School was moved to the Ellston Pioneer Center and is used as a museum facility. This school is open to students in the fall and on Saturday afternoons during the summer.

Another school relocated to Ellston is being used as a pool hall part of a bar.

Fifteen schools have been converted to homes, eight are used as farm buildings, seven are vacant, and four are used for storage.

Compiled by
Kathryne Sickels
305 South Pierce
Mount Ayr, Iowa 50854

Washington #8—Hazel Glen

Monroe #8—Jackson Hill

Interior of Monroe #8

Special activities were undertaken during Iowa's Sesquicentennial observance to preserve memories of country schools in Sac County.

Jackson #7 was restored and furnished with country school furnishings and moved to the Sac City Museum site at 13th and Main Street. A rededication ceremony was held on July 4.

The school is used annually by elementary students in Sac County to experience an old-fashioned school day.

The museum and school are open on Saturdays and Sundays from 2 - 4:30 p.m. from Memorial Day to Labor Day.

A booklet was also produced that included information about former Sac County country schools and written memories of former students and teachers. More than 170 persons provided material for the book, which was titled *Ring in the Memories*.

In 1913, there were 128 country schools with 2,118 students operating in the county. The valuation of those schools for that year was $62,180.

The majority of those schools have been torn down, but some have been converted to homes or are being used as farm buildings. An inventory of existing school buildings was not undertaken.

Two former schools have been converted to homes and one building is vacant.

Compiled by
Shirley Phillips
615 Main
Sac City, Iowa 50583

Jackson #7

Jackson #7 dedication

Some 44 one-room country schools have been identified in Scott County, including four maintained as museums.

Most of the former schools—26—have been converted to homes. Three are used as township halls and community centers, four are used as farm buildings, three are vacant, two are used as churches, one has been converted to an office, and one is used as a meeting place for the Hispanic Lulac Club.

The research compiled on country schools in Scott County by English teacher Dick Stahl resulted in a two-page feature story in the *Quad City Times,* which was picked up and distributed across the state by the Associated Press.

The museum schools include:

Davenport District #9—now located on the Mississippi Valley Fairgrounds, this school is open during the fair the first week in August, or by appointment by calling 319-226-5338.

Butler #3—is a replica of a school destroyed by fire in 1975. It is part of the William F. Cody (Buffalo Bill) boyhood home. Young Cody walked to this school with his sister. To reach this complex, take I-80 from Davenport, exit 301, turn left on Middle Road, go under I-80 to Z30. Turn left on Z30 and stay on that for 7 miles until it intersects with Bluff Road. Turn left and go about 1 1/2 miles. It is on the corner of Bluff Road and 230th Avenue. Call 319-225-2981. The Cody complex is open from April 1 through October 31.

Old Pleasant Hill School—enter LeClaire on Highway 67 going north and turn left on Territorial Road (F51) and go 1/2 mile. Teachers from the Pleasant Valley School District sometimes bring classes there so students can say they attended a one-room school. For more information, call Cecil Fletcher at 319-289-4413.

Long Grove, Butler #2—is now part of Walnut Grove Pioneer Village in Scott County Park located north of Davenport on Highway 61. Open from 9 a.m. to dusk with special events planned the last weekends in June, July, and August. Call 319-285-9903.

Schools converted to churches include Calvary Bible Church at the southeast corner of West Locust Street and Wisconsin Avenue in Davenport, and Victory Baptist Church at 5231 North Pine Street in Davenport.

Stone School, constructed in 1866 and located about a mile west of LeClaire, was placed on the National Register of Historic Places in 1978. It now stands vacant.

Compiled by
Dick Stahl
4702 Sheridan Street
Davenport, Iowa 52806

Another school is used as an office for a warehouse in Mt. Joy at the intersection of 209th and Brady Streets.

Probstei Independent

Old Pleasant Hill School

Blue Grass #7

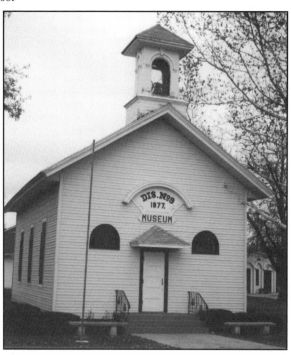

Davenport #9

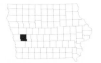

At least 12 one-room schools are still standing in Shelby County. Included in this group are the original Jackson #1 and a larger replacement for the original building. Both buildings are listed on the National Register of Historic Places.

The first Jackson #1 was built in 1884 for $642. It was later moved 1/4 mile west when the present one-room building was erected on the original site for $2,948 in 1923. The school doors were closed to students as a result of consolidation in 1958.

Reunions of former Jackson #1 students and teachers are held about every other year. The schools are being preserved by a farmer.

Jackson #5 is used as a township meeting hall and voting center.

Jackson #8 has been moved into Harlan and remodeled for use as a Seventh Day Adventist Church.

Fairview #2 is now being used as an antique shop in Corley.

Two schools from Polk Township have been converted to homes and two are being used as farm buildings.

Two other schools are now vacant and another is being used as a machine shed.

Compiled by
Mae M. Petersen
1103 Road M56
Harlan, Iowa 51537

The Shelby County Rural Teacher's Association, an organization of teachers who taught in one-room schools in the county, was formed in 1962. The group holds annual meetings in August.

Jackson #15—1917

Jackson #15—1997

Fairview #2

Washington #7—now in Panama

Four schools have been maintained as museums in the county. All of these schools are open during special community-wide observances and student groups have opportunities to spend time at each of the buildings.

The museum schools are located in Ireton near the elementary school, the county fairgrounds in Sioux Center, the historical village of Calliope on the edge of Hawarden, and across from the courthouse in Orange City.

Research conducted by the Sioux County Genealogical Society revealed two styles of country schools used in the county. The first buildings built between 1880 and 1900 were very simple, square box structures. Newer one-room schools constructed between 1920 and 1935 were cottage-type structures with windows on the south and east side.

Listed below is a summary of the type of schools and the way they are presently being used:

- schools now vacant located on the original sites—new 5—old 2
- schools located on original sites remodeled into homes—new 9
- schools moved and remodeled into homes—new 21—old 4
- schools moved and remodeled into farm buildings—new 10—old 4
- schools moved and used as museums—new 3—old 1
- schools moved and used for storage—new 1—old 1
- schools moved and remodeled into boutiques—new 2

The Sioux County researchers also were able to trace how the lumber from 21 schools that were dismantled was used: seven were rebuilt as homes, 13 were rebuilt as farm buildings, and one was used for a new garage.

The two boutiques are Simple Pleasures Tea House located at 2835 440th Street near Maurice; and The Country School, an antique and craft store, 3070 360th Street, Sioux Center.

Compiled by
Mrs. Jennie Den Besten
2468 270th Street
Rock Valley, Iowa 51247

Eagle #1

Scott School—now a museum in Calliope

Museum in Orange City

Museum in Ireton

Grant #2

In 1902 there were 129 one-room schools in Story County. By 1935-36 that number had been reduced to 23. The last one-room school in the county ceased operation in 1953.

The four museums in the county include the Hoggatt School, which was relocated to the Meeker School grounds on 20th Street and Burnett, and is now used to give Ames elementary students a country school experience. Furnishings from three other Ames area one-room schools are housed in Hoggart.

Sheldall School is now located in Story City across from the swimming pool, just south of the high school. This school is maintained by the Story City Historical Society and is open sundays from Memorial Day to Labor Day, 1-5 p.m., and during the annual Scandinavian Days Festival in early June.

The Halley School is located on the 4-H Fairgrounds in Nevada. This 1874 school was restored and is maintained by the Nevada Community Historical Society. For viewing, phone 515-382-4876.

Another unique museum-type complex is Frontier Acres created by Jo Ann Twedt of rural Roland. She has developed a pioneer prairie train on an acreage where she lives with her husband. Twedt engages visitors in a variety of programs focusing on pioneer and early settler life. This area includes replicas of covered wagons, an Indian wickiup, log cabin, general store, train car, and a country schoolhouse with authentic furnishings. For information about the Frontier Acres complex, call 515-388-4022.

The former Thorson School has been converted into a museum for the community of Roland. A basement and an additional room have been added to the schoolhouse with a variety of items and displays, including some country school pieces. Hours for the museum are determined annually by the Roland Historical Society, usually each or rotating Sunday afternoons during the summer.

The town of Maxwell has an extensive museum which features items from former country schools in the area. For information contact museum curator Jesse Farr at 515-387-8832.

Compiled by
Joa LaVille
117 West Ash, Box 516
Roland, Iowa 50236

It is estimated that 34 country schools have been converted to homes, 13 are being used as various types of farm buildings, and two are vacant.

Hoggatt School

Halley School

Sheldall School

Lafayette Township—now in Story City

229

A country school in Tama County was a candidate for destruction when Rob and Jan Webster decided to purchase Pleasant Hill #6 and restore it.

The school was moved approximately four miles to the Webster's farm in July of 1997 and restoration is now underway. The Websters plan to restore the upper main floor of the 30' by 32' building close to its original condition. The basement will be developed as a country getaway home. Marie Vileta, who used to teach at the school, is advising the Websters on the planned restoration.

Ellen Young, a reporter at the *Traer Star Clipper* who helped compile information about schools in Tama County, provided these facts about Tama County country schools in 1880:

- there were 172 schools—163 frame, six brick, and three stone
- the value of the buildings was $133,399; and the value of school equipment, including 59 library books, was $1,854
- there were 5,853 students enrolled in the country schools; attendance averaged 3,422
- there were 336 teachers—115 male and 221 female, the approximate ratio in Iowa today
- male teachers were being paid $31.19 per month, and female teachers $25.54 per month
- average tuition cost per pupil was $1.65 per month

Compiled by
Ellen Young, editor
Traer Star Clipper
2nd Street
Traer, Iowa 50675
and Lavonne Jacobsen
509 W. 7th Street
Tama, Iowa 52339

One former country school in Tama County continues to be used as a township center and polling place. It is Richland #5 located southeast of Tama near the village of Haven.

Usage for the other schools remaining in the county include eight farm buildings, eight homes, two garages, one storage building, and four are vacant.

Carroll #1

Crystal #2

Crystal #5

About the turn of the century there were 121 one-room schools operating in Taylor County. A few years later that number increased to 130. Reorganization in 1958 closed the few remaining one-room schools.

Today, 33 one-room school buildings remain in the county. Clayton #3, known as the Hess School, has been restored and relocated to the Taylor County Museum grounds located on the northwest edge of Bedford. The school is fully furnished and used by student groups.

The Daugherty School, or Benton #2, remains at its original location and is used as an art studio by Michael Bose. It is located west of Bedford at 1904 265th Street.

Another well-maintained school located on the original site is the Valley School, Polk #4. The school, which is owned by S.K. Mendenhall, retains many of its original furnishings. It is located south of Bedford near the Missouri state line. This building may be the most southern well-maintained country school in Iowa.

An unusual event happened at Holt #7 when a baby girl was born on March 22, 1877. Nettie Dunkin was brought into the world at the school because a fire forced her parents to vacate their home a few hours before she was born. This school is now being used as a farm building.

Former Iowa Governor and U.S. Senator Bourke B. Hickenlooper started his education at Gay #8 in Taylor County.

Eleven former schools are now vacant, seven are used as farm buildings, seven for storage, four for homes, and one as a township meeting place.

Compiled by
Helen Janson
and the Taylor County
Genealogy Society
P.O. Box 8
Gravity, Iowa 50848

Grove #6

Marshall #4

Clayton #3 (background)

Daugherty School

233

Some 23 former one-room schools are still standing in Union County.

Lincoln #5, which operated as a school for 94 years and was the last rural school open in the county was relocated to McKinley Park in Creston where it is maintained as a country school museum. Classes are conducted in the spring for area students. The school is part of an 11-building heritage complex operated by the Union County Historical Society. The complex is open seven days a week from 1 - 5 p.m., June - August. It can be open by appointment by contacting Marcella Howe, 515-782-4247 or Jane Briley, 515-782-4525.

Two other schools are also being preserved. Jones #3, Riverdale School, was relocated to the Mount Pisgah Mormon Trail historic site south of Lorimor. An individual is also restoring the Prairie Star School in Platte Township in the southwest corner of Union County.

In the town of Cromwell, two schools are being combined to create a home. Dodge #6 has been converted into a Christian Church near Lorimor and Highland #5 is used for voting and 4-H meetings.

Some 11 schools are being utilized as homes, six are vacant, and two others are used for storage.

Compiled by
Marcella Howe
1101 North Vine
Creston, Iowa 50801

New Hope #3

Dodge #7

Highland #5

Highland #7

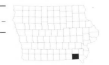

A former country school—Winchester— is now being used as the central administrative offices for the Van Buren Community School District in Keosauqua.

Five other schools have been preserved as museum-type facilities. Valley #3 is located in the memorial park in Leando beside the elementary school. This school is open for individuals or groups to tour. It is also used by elementary students. Call 515-963-4322 or 515-936-7117.

Another school maintained by the neighborhood and used as a meeting place and museum is Oak Grove. It is located beside an 1895 church and is west of Douds on Highway 16 and 2 miles south on Oak Grove Road.

Another museum school, Ellis, is located at 718 Dodge Street in Keosauqua. It is located near the Pearson House which served as an underground railroad facility. These buildings are maintained by the Van Buren Historical Society and are open on Sundays, 1-4 p.m., May through October.

The East Union #3 has been relocated to Morris Memorial Park. This area is used for camping, picnicking, fishing, and hiking. The park includes six other buildings besides the school, and a 60-acre pond.

The Bennett School is owned and preserved by the Bennett Community School near Birmingham. Monthly meetings and a homecoming celebration are held at the school in the fall.

Utica #3 was relocated on the main street in Stockport. It was used as a craft shop.

At least two other schools have been converted to homes and two buildings are vacant.

Compiled by
Nell Swygard
past president of the
Van Buren Historical Society
105 W. Adams
Fairfield, Iowa 52556

Utica #3

Stone School

Winchester—now Administration Hdqtrs. Van Buren School District

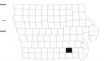

In 1921 there were 95 one-room schools operating in Wapello County. Today there are at least 26 country schools still standing in the county and efforts are underway to restore one school and maintain it as a turn-of-the-century school.

Ed and Deb Miller are working to restore Wellman #1 at Cooperhead Road and 205th Street east of Blakesburg off Highway 147. The school features a unique wraparound porch with the original well that is still operational. A new roof and windows, plus a replacement bell have been recently added to the school.

Another important school in the past history of the county is Dahlonega #1. Three schools have been built at this location beginning with a log cabin in the early 1800s. The town of Dahlonega grew up around the school and was once bigger than Ottumwa. Now the only structure remaining in this once thriving community is the school, which is in good condition but vacant.

A dramatic event occurred in April of 1990 when Brush Creek #4 was struck by lightning and burned to the ground (see photo).

Included among the 26 schools in the county today are ten converted to homes, two being used as farm buildings, and two being used as garages. Another school is being used for storage and ten are vacant.

One of the more ambitious country school publishing projects was undertaken in 1994 by the Ottumwa Public Library and a team of country school promoters. They produced an 880-page, hardcover book that included pictures of most of the schools that once existed in the county, plus names of students and teachers for each year the schools were in operation. A companion softcover booklet of Wapello County Township maps in 1908 identified locations for all country schools operating that year.

Compiled by
Charles L. Swanson
53 Kingsley Drive
Ottumwa, Iowa 52501

Wellman #1—1950s

Wellman #1—1997

Pleasant Home School

Brush Creek #4 fire

Research revealed that in 1902 there were 138 one-room rural schools operating in Warren County. In August of 1997, information was obtained on 26 one-room schools still standing in the county.

The Mt. Hope School was relocated to the Warren County Fairgrounds in 1967 and has been maintained since then as a country school museum by the Warren County Historical Society and the Fair Board. It is part of a historic village complex that includes a general store, pioneer church, log cabin, and history museum. Classes are conducted for Indianola elementary students in May and the complex is open during the fair and on Sunday afternoons May through September. It is located on the west edge of Indianola on Highway 92.

Another school, Belmont Center, is in the process of being developed into a community museum by the Milo Development Corporation.

U.S. Senator Tom Harkin attended the Cumming one-room school. That building is now being used as a restaurant called Adam and Abby's. It is located 4 miles west of Norwalk on Highway G14.

The Hoosier Row school is now used as a community center. In 1996, the White Oak Climber 4-H club and Hoosier Row Community Center club obtained a 4-H Sesquicentennial grant to help pay for re-siding the school.

Some 11 schools have been converted to homes, eight are being used as farm buildings, two are vacant, and one is being used for storage.

Another school that had been converted to a home—Summerset—was destroyed by fire January 4, 1997. Former students of the school held reunions, which will be continued.

Compiled by
Maxine Henry
2490 50th Avenue
New Virginia, Iowa 50210

Cumming School—now restaurant   *Photo by Jolene Rosauer*

Hoosier Row School

Mt. Hope School

Research by the Washington County Historical Society has identified 44 former one-room schools that are remaining in the county.

Three of the schools are operated as museums. Straw College, or Summit School, has been relocated to the Kalona Heritage Village. Students who attended say their school was nicknamed "Straw College" because during the winter, straw was stuffed behind the wainscotting for warmth. The school is one of 11 buildings in the village complex. The complex is open during the summer from 10 a.m. - 4 p.m. and in the winter months from 11 a.m. - 3 p.m. An admission is charged.

Another school maintained as a museum is the Smith Creek School. It is located in the Wellman Historical Park on 7th Avenue and is maintained by the Wellman Historical Society. Old-fashioned country school classes are held at the school, and a "Grandparents' Day" program is also held at the school. Scout troops have helped keep the area clean and have done plantings around the school. Elementary students have done painting at the school. Area clubs use the school for special meetings.

The Walnut Creek School is maintained as a museum by the Washington County Historical Society. The school contains much of its original furnishings, complete with teacher's hand bell and a working outdoor pump. An open house is held at the school in June and many attend in turn-of-the-century clothing. The school is located 7 miles southwest of Washington on Highway 1.

Another school that remains in good condition, and is maintained in its original condition by an individual, is the "red brick" school. It was in operation from 1850-1956. It is located 2 miles south of Washington on W55.

Several years ago two country schools—Living Lake and South Prairie—were relocated to the Washington County Fairgrounds. The schools were combined into a building that is now used as an administrative office and Red Cross emergency center.

Another school—Greenvale—is used as a bait and grocery store near Lake Darling in Clay Township.

Amish operate four one-room schools in the county, 17 are used for storage, nine have been converted to homes, and six are vacant.

Compiled by
Charles Hotle, Mary
Zielinski, Mary Levy, and
the Washington County
Historical Society
Box 364
Washington, Iowa 52353

Pleasant Valley—Amish School

Smith Creek School

Straw College

243

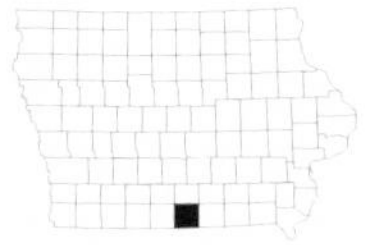

At one time there were 122—now there are at least 14 country schools still remaining in Wayne County.

The "Little Red Schoolhouse," formerly called Pleasant Hill and Tickle Grass, is operated as a museum by the Wayne County Historical Society. At the urging of that group, the Iowa Department of Transportation designated the area surrounding the school as a roadside park. Trees were planted, the county conservation board provided picnic tables, REA provided plug-ins and electricity for the area. Lions Club members and 4-H members recently repainted the school. Volunteers from Lineville open the school for public viewing from 2-4 p.m. Sunday afternoons during June, July, and August. The school is located 3 miles north of Lineville on Highway 65.

Another one-room school from the Harvard area has been moved to the International Center for Rural Culture and Art, 1 mile east of Allerton. It will be restored as a museum and be featured with a historic round barn and the Spring Branch Church.

Clio #6 is used as a Head Start center in Allerton. Annual school reunions are held at the Hickory Ridge School in Wright Township. Elm School was moved to the Lineville-Clio school grounds and is now used for storage and the teachers' lounge.

Six other buildings are vacant. Two others are used as farm buildings and one is a township community center.

Compiled by
Josephine Johnson
RR#2 Box 339
Lineville, Iowa 50147

Lewisburg—Clay Township

Elm School—formerly used by Lineville-Clio School District

Williams School—future museum

Pleasant Hill School

One hundred and seventy country schools once dotted the prairies and woodlands of Webster County. These quaint classrooms were located every two miles, with an average of nine such structures in each of the county's 20 townships.

The county's first one-room public school was erected in 1857 near the pioneer community of Border Plains, located in the east-central region of the county. Today, a small cemetery is the only remaining hint of this once budding community. The original wooden schoolhouse has been preserved, extensively furnished with authentic relics of rural education, and relocated to the grounds of the Fort Museum and Frontier Village in the county seat of Fort Dodge. The museum complex is open seven days a week from 9 - 6 p.m., starting the last week in April through October. The museum is located on the western edge of Fort Dodge off Highway 169.

The last rural school operating in Webster County closed in 1966 and was located in the tiny town of Evanston. Evanston was coincidentally located just two miles north of the Border Plains site where the county's rural education seeds were first planted more than a century earlier.

Recent research accumulated photos of nine structures that still maintain the one-room country school appearance. However, the buildings are now serving diverse purposes—ranging from homes and storage sheds to a museum (as mentioned above) and even a garage. It is even rumored that part of the Dayton Country Club was made from an area country school building.

It is estimated that additional school buildings remain in other areas of the county, bringing the approximate number of one-room structures that still exist in some shape or form, at original or new locations, to roughly 25.

Currently the only known brick country school, built in 1916, is for sale. The building was once part of the community of Otho, but was left behind to serve as a country school when the town picked up and moved two miles to the northwest in order to be located near the railroad.

A wooden-frame school was recently auctioned off in May of 1997. The one-room building had most recently served as a voting precinct, but will now be moved and used for storage on a farm just a few miles from its original location.

Badger School is one of the few two-room, ground level school buildings remaining in the state. It is now used as a residence.

Compiled by
Deann Hayden-Luke
2172 290th Street
Fort Dodge, Iowa 50501

In 1997 a three-part series of articles about one-room schools appeared in the *Today* magazine formerly published by the Iowa Central Community College at Fort Dodge.

Border Plains School

Badger School   *Photo by Jack Grandgeorge*

Evanston School   *Photo by* The Today Magazine, *Fort Dodge*

Information was obtained about 42 one-room schools once operating in the county. But there are 28 "mystery schools," including one or more from each township, that no one was able to describe what happened to them.

One school—a second Linden #5—was moved to the county fairgrounds in Thompson on June 25, 1996, to be restored as a museum for a sesquicentennial project. The school is being managed by the Winnebago County Historical Society and the county fair board. The first Linden #5 was moved into Thompson in the 1930s and converted to a home.

Two other schools were moved from the county to be used as museum buildings. The Junction School, formerly located 2 miles north of Forest City, was relocated to the Mason City Airport; and a square, one-room school was moved to the "Farming of Yesteryear" museum area near Kiester, Minnesota.

A bell from the Haugland School in Center Township was given to a missionary who is using it in Cameroun, Africa.

Compiled by
Maxine Olson
P.O. Box 62
Leland, Iowa 50453

Nine schools have been converted to various types of farm buildings—sheds, shops, and grain bins. Four are being used as garages, and one is used as a township meeting center and voting place. At least 25 one-room schools have been converted to homes.

Linden #5

Forest #6—museum moved near Mason City airport

New Linden #5 before being moved

Old Linden #5

During the springs of 1985 and 1986, the Winneshiek County Historical Society conducted a site survey of rural schools in Winneshiek County. The results of these surveys indicated that 55 schoolhouses were found on their original sites, 35 were relocated, and 55 buildings had been razed. The survey used as its basis for research a 1933 plat map of the county kept by the county superintendent to use when he visited the schools. In the mid-1930s there were 145 rural schools in use. By 1960, the last rural school year, only 24 were in operation.

The rural school survey found that 17 out of the 20 townships contained existing rural schoolhouses. Of the existing 55 sites, 20 are vacant, 16 are residences, six serve as township halls, ten are farm outbuildings, two are listed on the National Register of Historic Places, and one serves as a church.

The adaptive use of schools removed from their original sites include: two vacant, ten residences, nine shop/garages, five storage facilities, and two businesses. The survey found the buildings' fabric included: 72 frame, seven brick, five stucco, and three cement block structures. The last school was built in the county in 1947. This school featured cement block walls, poured concrete basement, automatic oil furnace, indoor toilets, electric lights, and a modern kitchen. Unfortunately, over the past ten years since the completion of the rural school survey about ten additional sites have vanished from the county landscape. There were an estimated 80 country schools in the county in 1997.

Some of the historical country schools in the county are readily available to tourists. The Winneshiek County Historical Society operates the Locust School located in Pleasant Township 10 miles north of Decorah on County Highway W38. Listed on the National Register of Historic Places in 1978, the Locust School was in continuous operation for 106 years, reportedly an Iowa record for a school building on its original site. It was built in 1854 of locally quarried limestone. Until 1856, when other log schools were built, the Locust School was the only school north of Decorah, and at one time there were 70-80 pupils attending the school. Beginning in 1950, the school ceased being an "all-grades" school and instead served specific grade levels until it closed in 1960. The school is open on weekends, Memorial Day through Labor Day, 1-4 p.m.

A popular building in the county is the Highlandville School located 20 miles northeast of Decorah on County Highway A24. The present white-painted frame structure, built in 1911, was erected on the same foundation of an earlier school which had been destroyed by fire. The school has two classrooms for dividing the different grades. The building is presently used as the township hall and as a dance hall. During the summer and fall, live performers play old-time music for these community events.

Listed on the National Register of Historic Places, the Frankville School is located on State Street in Frankville. Built in 1972, this school is a well-preserved example of mid-19th century vernacular stonemasonry. The two-story schoolhouse served the Frankville community until 1962. From 1965 to 1984, the Winneshiek County Historical Society operated the

Compiled by
Steve Johnson
2984 River Road
Decorah, Iowa 52101

building as a county museum. It was then deeded over to the Winneshiek County Conservation Commission to be used as a community center.

The Bouska Log School was the first school for the Bohemian immigrants who settled in the Spillville area. The schoolhouse design is similar to the dog trot or breezeway log homes from the southern states. The two, single-story log rooms were connected by a central frame hallway. It was built in 1853 by Martin Bouska, one of the first Bohemian settlers in the county. He was a teacher in the old country and ran a private school for early immigrants. The schoolhouse has been removed from its original site and is presently used as a visitors' center by the Bily Clock Museum in Spillville.

As part of the Decorah Vesterheim Museum's Open-Air Division, the Rovang Parochial School is typical of the many log schoolhouses which were found in the Midwest. Open to the public during the summer season, the school was built by members of the Washington Prairie congregation. It was not built for the "3 Rs" but for the "4th R," religion. The structure was believed to have been built in 1879. The school had a stove for heating the building at the back, near the door. There were three windows on each side and a kerosene lamp with reflectors to provide some lighting. A "blackboard" was literally that, consisting of two boards painted black behind the teacher's desk in the front of the room.

Locust School

Frankville School

Burr Oak School

In 1902 there were 167 one-room schools operating in Woodbury County. In 1997 there were at least 47 one-room schools in the county. Included are eight museums.

For more than 20 years, members of the Sioux City Junior League have conducted 1886-style classes for Sioux City elementary students. Classes are held in an authentic one-room school moved from near Holstein in 1976 as a Bicentennial project undertaken by the TOY National Bank and the Junior League. The school is located at 3601 Country Club Boulevard across from Hoover Middle School. A key to the school can be obtained from the Hoover administrative office.

Three schools have been relocated to the Woodbury Fairgrounds east of Moville. Wolf Creek #5 is used as a school. Elementary students attend classes there in the spring. Concord #5 is used as a general store and Little Egypt is used as a post office at the fair.

Summit #2 is another museum school that is located in Little Sioux Park south of Correctionville. The school is open from Memorial Day to Labor Day on Sunday afternoons from 2-4 p.m. by the Good Hope Club. Classes from three area schools attend country school classes at this school each spring.

Another school from Moville Township was moved to Copeland Park south of Correctionville near the Little Sioux River. A special country program is conducted at this school on the 4th of July.

Another building that has been part of Sioux City's history since 1875 is the Sherwin Land Office School. It was first used as a real estate office and later as a church. In 1879 the school board rented the building and used it as a school for more than a decade. Today this building is located in Riverside Park on Riverside Boulevard north of Interstate 29.

The LaCroix School is now used as a lodge by the Lakeport Gun Club. It's located 1 1/2 miles north of Sloan.

Some 22 schools have been converted to homes including ten in Moville. When the three museum schools at the fairgrounds are included in this total, it makes Moville the town with the most one-room school buildings in Iowa.

Some 13 of the former one-room schools are now being used as farm buildings, three have been converted to garages, and one building is vacant.

Norm Ashby was assisted by Sarah McElrath of Moville, Marjorie E. Hoppe of Correctionville, and Fayann Hubert of Salix.

Compiled by
Norm Ashby
2712 Magnolia Court
Sioux City, Iowa 51106

Copeland Park

Fairview School

Wolfcreek #5   *Photo by Moville Record*

253

Worth County probably has the highest percentage of country schools used in the early 1900s still standing. Information from a 1913 plat map shows locations for 88 country schools that were operating that year.

Research done by Beverly Madsen of Northwood during the winter and spring of 1997 identified 81 country schools still standing in Worth County. Some of those schools were moved in from other counties and some were replacement schools built in the 1920s and 1930s.

More than half of these schools—43—have been converted to homes. Some 21 are being used as farm buildings, eight are standing vacant, four are being used as garages, two are being used as businesses, one is used as an American Legion Hall in Grafton, one has been moved and converted into a church used as an African American congregation in Manly.

The museum, known as Swensrud School, was built in 1874 on a farm northeast of Northwood. In 1972, it was moved to Central Park at the junction of Highways 65 and 105 south of Northwood. The school contains rows of desks with carvings of long ago, a pot-bellied stove, lunch pails on the bench, and a collection of old school books. Names of teachers who taught in this school are posted on the wall.

Compiled by
Beverly Madsen
4725 Juniper Avenue
Northwood, Iowa 50459

This school is open Sundays from 2 to 4 p.m. Memorial Day through Labor Day.

Swensrud School

Swensrud interior

Wright County's most significant country school—Lake Township #6—played an important role in the development of the 4-H movement. An incident at the school led to the creation of the 4-H Club emblem.

When County Superintendent of Schools O.H. Benson visited the school, students presented him with a bouquet of "good luck" in the form of several four-leaf clovers they had picked up at recess.

That incident sparked an idea with Benson that led to the creation of the 4-H symbol that is still in use. Benson went on to work with the U.S. Department of Agriculture as director of boys' and girls' club work and helped spread the 4-H program across the United States.

Today, Lake Township #6 is used as a museum to document the early days of the 4-H movement and is dedicated to the memory of Benson. It is located in the Clarion City Park on Highway 3. It is open to the public during the summer. Many families have picnic lunches at this park. The school can be seen at other times by contacting the Clarion Area Chamber of Commerce or the Wright County Extension Service.

Iowa Township #4 was moved to River Park in Belmond on Highway 69, 1 1/2 blocks south of Main Street. It was restored as a museum school by the Belmond Historical Society.

When Wall Lake #5 was closed, it became a polling place and a township community center. It is still furnished as it was when used as a school. It is open on request by contacting Gerald Blackman, 515-532-3072.

Five other former schools are vacant, at least two have been converted to homes, and two are being used as farm buildings.

Compiled by
Louise Mock
615 5th Avenue NE
Clarion, Iowa 50525

Wall Lake #5

Holmes—two-room school

The Old Country School
by Ethelyn Kincher

How strange the silent schoolhouse seems
Alone here on the hill;
The district bus has passed it by
The old brass bell is still.

The weed grown yard and silent swings
Are lonely in the sun;
These warm spring days are long and bright
But the children have not come.

The knife scarred desks and aging floors
Betray with dust and grime;
That the old country school is now
A monument to time.

But in the hearts to all who have
A country legacy;
The district school will always be
As near as memory.

This was written by a Sac County parent and given to a teacher at the time of a country school closing—from *"Ring in the Memories,"* a history of Sac County country schools.

Sunnyside School, Emmet County, at the turn of the century